HOUSEKEEPING vs. THE DIRT

HOUSEKEEPING

vs.

THE DIRT

BY

NICK HORNBY

BELIEVER BOOKS

a tiny division of

MCSWEENEY'S
which is also tiny

BELIEVER BOOKS
a division of
McSWEENEY'S

849 Valencia Street
San Francisco, CA 94110

books.believermag.com

Cover design by Sam Potts, Inc.

Printed in Canada by Westcan Printing Group.

ISBN: 1-932416-59-5
978-1-932416-59-6

For Dave and Serge, who rock'n'read.

TABLE OF CONTENTS

PREFACE

I began writing this column in the summer of 2003. It seemed to me that what I had chosen to read in the preceding few weeks contained a narrative, of sorts—that one book led to another, and thus themes and patterns emerged, patterns that might be worth looking at. And, of course, that was pretty much the last time my reading had any kind of logic or shape to it. Ever since then my choice of books has been haphazard, whimsical, and entirely shapeless.

It still seemed like a fun thing to do, though, writing about reading, as opposed to writing about individual books. At the beginning of my writing career I reviewed a lot of fiction, but I had to pretend, as reviewers do, that I had read the books outside of space, time, and self—in other words, I had to pretend that I hadn't read them when I was tired and grumpy, or drunk, that I wasn't envious of the author, that I had no agenda, no personal aesthetic or personal taste or personal problems, that I hadn't read other reviews of the same book already, that I didn't know who the author's friends and enemies were, that I wasn't trying to place a book with the same publisher, that I hadn't been bought lunch by the book's doe-eyed publicist. Most of all I had to pretend that I hadn't written the review because I was urgently in need of a quick couple of hundred quid. Being paid to read a book and then write about it creates a dynamic which compromises the reviewer in all kinds of ways, very few of them helpful.

So this column was going to be different. Yes, I would be paid for it, but I would be paid to write about what I would have done anyway, which was read the books I wanted to read. And if I felt that mood, morale, concentration levels, weather, or family history had affected my relationship with a book, I could and would say so. Inevitably, however, the knowledge that I had to write something for the *Believer* at the end of each month changed my reading habits profoundly. For a start, I probably read more books than I might otherwise have done. I suspect that I used to take a longer break between books, a couple of days, maybe, during which time I'd carry a copy of the *New Yorker* or *Mojo* around with me, but now I push on with the next book, scared I won't have enough to write about (or that I'll look bad, unbookish and unworthy of the space in a publication as smart as the *Believer*). Magazines have been the real casualties of this regime (although the *Economist* has survived, partly to replace the newspapers I'm not reading.)

It was the very nature of the *Believer* itself, however, that really shook up my reading, hopefully forever. The magazine, which is five months older than the column, is a broad church, and all sorts of writers (and artists, and filmmakers, and other creative types) are welcome to stand in the pulpit and preach, but it has one commandment: THOU SHALT NOT SLAG ANYONE OFF. As I understand it, the founders of the magazine wanted one place, one tiny corner of the world, in which writers could be sure that they weren't going to get a kicking; predictably and depressingly, this ambition was mocked mercilessly, mostly by those critics whose children would go hungry if their parents weren't able to abuse authors whose books they didn't much like.

I understood and supported the magazine's stance, which seemed admirable and entirely unproblematic to me—until I had to write about the books I'd read which I hadn't much liked. The first couple of times this happened, earnest discussions took place with the magazine's editors, who felt that I'd crossed a line, and I either rewrote the offending passages so that I struck a more conciliatory tone, or the offending books and writers became anonymous. I didn't mind in the least, and in any case it gave me the opportunity to mock the *Believer's* ambition mercilessly. (For the record: there is no Polysyllabic Spree. I deal with Vendela Vida and Andrew Leland, co-editor and managing editor of the *Believer,* respectively, and they are neither humorless nor evangelical. They even watch television, I think.)

The *Believer's* ethos did, however, make me think about what and why I read. I didn't want to keep rewriting offending passages in my columns, and I certainly didn't want to keep using the phrases *Anonymous writer* or *Unnameable novel*. So what to do? My solution was to try to choose books I knew I would like. I'm not sure this idea is as blindingly obvious as it seems. We often read books that we think we ought to read, or that we think we ought to have read, or that other people think we should read (I'm always coming across people who have a mental, sometimes even an actual, list of the books they think they should have read by the time they turn forty, fifty, or dead); I'm sure I'm not the only one who harrumphs his way through a highly praised novel, astonished but actually rather pleased that so many people have got it so wrong. As a consequence, the first thing to be cut from my reading diet was contemporary literary fiction. This seems to me to be the highest-risk category—or the highest risk for me, at any rate, given my tastes.

I am not particularly interested in language. Or rather, I am interested in what language can do for me, and I spend many hours each day trying to ensure that my prose is as simple as it can possibly be. But I do not wish to produce prose that draws attention to itself, rather than the world it describes, and I certainly don't have the patience to read it. (I suspect that I'm not alone here. That kind of writing tends to be admired by critics more than by book buyers, if the best-seller lists can be admitted as evidence: the literary novels that have reached a mass audience over the last decade or so usually ask readers to look through a relatively clear pane of glass at their characters.) I am not attempting to argue that the books I like are "better" than more opaquely written novels; I am simply pointing out my own tastes and limitations as a reader. To put it crudely, I get bored, and when I get bored I tend to get tetchy. It has proved surprisingly easy to eliminate boredom from my reading life.

And boredom, let's face it, is a problem that many of us have come to associate with books. It's one of the reasons why we choose to do almost anything else rather than read; very few of us pick up a book after the children are in bed and the dinner has been made and the dirty dishes cleared away. We'd rather turn on the television. Some evenings we'd rather go to all the trouble of getting into a car and driving to a cinema, or waiting for a bus that might take us somewhere near one. This is partly because reading appears to be more effortful than watching TV, and usually it is, although if you choose to watch one of the HBO series, such as *The Sopranos* or *The Wire,* then it's a close-run thing, because the plotting in these programs, the speed and complexity of the dialogue, are as demanding as a lot of the very best fiction.

One of the problems, it seems to me, is that we have got it into our heads that books should be hard work, and that unless they're hard work, they're not doing us any good. I recently had conversations with two friends, both of whom were reading a very long political biography that had appeared in many of 2005's "Books of the Year" lists. They were struggling. Both of these people are parents—they each, coincidentally, have three children—and both have demanding full-time jobs. And each night, in the few minutes they allowed themselves to read before sleep, they plowed gamely though a few paragraphs about the (very) early years of a major twentieth-century world figure. At the rate of progress they were describing, it would take them many, many months before they finished the book, possibly even decades. (One of them told me that he'd put it down for a couple of weeks, and on picking it up again was extremely excited to see that the bookmark was much deeper into the book than he'd dared hope. He then realized that one of his kids had dropped it and put the bookmark back in the wrong place. He was crushed.) The truth is, of course, that neither of them will ever finish it—or at least, not in this phase of their lives. In the process, though, they will have reinforced a learned association of books with struggle.

I am not trying to say that the book itself was the cause of this anguish. I can imagine other people racing through it, and I can certainly imagine these two people racing through books that others might find equally daunting. It seems clear to me, though, that the combination of that book with these readers at this stage in their lives is not a happy one. If reading books is to survive as a leisure activity—and there are statistics which show that this is by no means assured—then we have to promote the joys of reading rather than the (dubious) benefits. I would never attempt to dissuade anyone from reading a book. But please, if you're reading a book that's killing you, put it down and read something else, just as you would reach for the remote if you weren't enjoying a TV program. Your failure to enjoy a highly rated novel doesn't mean you're dim—you may find that Graham Greene is more to your taste, or Stephen Hawking, or Iris Murdoch, or Ian Rankin. Dickens, Stephen King, whoever. It doesn't matter. All I know is that you can get very little from a book that is making you weep with the effort of reading it. You won't remember it, and you'll learn nothing from it, and you'll be less likely to choose a book over *Big Brother* next time you have a choice.

"If reading is a workout for the mind, then Britain must be buzzing with intellectual energy," said one sarcastic columnist in the *Guardian*. "Train stations have shops packed with enough words to keep even the most muscular brain engaged for weeks. Indeed, the carriages are full of people exercising their intellects the full length of their journeys. Yet somehow, the fact that millions daily devour thousands of words from *Hello,* the *Sun, The Da Vinci Code, Nuts,* and so on does not inspire the hope that the average cerebrum is in excellent health. It's not just that you read, it's what you read that counts." This sort of thing—and it's a regrettably common sneer in our broadsheet newspapers—must drive school librarians, publishers, and literacy campaigners nuts. In Britain, more than twelve million adults have a reading age of thirteen or under, and yet some clever-dick journalist still insists on telling us that unless we're reading something *proper,* then we might as well not bother at all.

But what's proper? Whose books will make us more intelligent? Not mine, that's for sure. But has Ian McEwan got the right stuff? Julian Barnes? Jane Austen, Zadie Smith, E. M. Forster? Hardy or Dickens? Those Dickens readers who famously waited on the dockside in New York for news of Little Nell—were they hoping to be educated? Dickens is Literary now, of course, because the books are old. But his work has survived not because he makes you think, but because he makes you feel, and he makes you laugh, and you need to know what is going to happen to his characters. I have on my desk here a James Lee Burke novel, a thriller in the Dave Robicheaux series, which sports on its covers ringing endorsements from the *Literary Review,* the *Guardian,* and the *Independent* on Sunday, so there's a possibility that somebody who writes for a broadsheet might approve.... Any chance of this giving my gray matter a workout? How much of a stretch is it for a nuclear physicist to read a book on nuclear physics? How much cleverer will we be if we read *Of Mice and Men,* Steinbeck's beautiful, simple novella? Or Tobias Wolff's brilliant *This Boy's Life,* or *Lucky Jim,* or *To Kill a Mockingbird*? Enormous intelligence has gone into the creation of all of these books, just as it has into the creation of the iPod, but the intelligence is not transferable. It's there to serve a purpose.

But there it is. It's set in stone, apparently: books must be hard work; otherwise they're a waste of time. And so we grind our way through serious, and sometimes seriously dull, novels, or enormous biographies of political figures, and every time we do so, books come to seem a little more like a duty, and *Pop Idol* starts to look a little more attractive. Please, please, put it down.

And please, please stop patronizing those who are reading a book—*The Da Vinci Code,* maybe—because they are enjoying it. For a start, none of us knows what kind of an effort this represents for the individual reader. It could be his or her first full-length adult novel; it might be the book that finally reveals the purpose and joy of reading to someone who has hitherto been mystified by the attraction books exert on others. And anyway, reading for enjoyment is what we should all be doing. I don't mean we should all be reading chick lit or thrillers (although if that's what you want to read, it's fine by me, because here's something else no one will ever tell you: if you don't read the classics, or the novel that won this year's Booker Prize, then *nothing bad will happen to you;* more importantly, *nothing good will happen to you if you do*); I simply mean that turning pages should not be like walking through thick mud. The whole purpose of books is that we read them, and if you find you can't, it might not be *your* inadequacy that's to blame. "Good" books can be pretty awful sometimes.

The regrettable thing about the culture war we still, after all these years, seem to be fighting is that it divides books into two camps: the trashy and the worthwhile. No one who is paid to talk about books for a living seems to be able to convey the message that this isn't how it works, that "good" books can provide every bit as much pleasure as "trashy" ones. Why worry about that if there's no difference anyway? Because it gives you more choice. You may not have to read about conspiracies, or the romantic tribulations of thirtysomething women, in order to be entertained. You may find that you're enthralled by Anthony Beevor's *Stalingrad,* or Donna Tartt's *The Secret History,* or *Great Expectations.* Read anything, as long as you can't wait to pick it up again.

I'm a reader for lots of reasons. On the whole, I tend to hang out with readers, and I'm scared they wouldn't want to hang out with me if I stopped. (They're interesting people, and they know a lot of interesting things, and I'd miss them.) I'm a writer, and I need to read, for inspiration and education and because I want to get better, and only books can teach me how. Sometimes, yes, I read to find things out—as I get older, I feel my ignorance weighing more heavily on me. I want to know what it's like to be him or her, to live there or then. I love the detail about the workings of the human heart and mind that only fiction can provide—film can't get in close enough. But the most important reason of all, I think, is this. When I was nine years old, I spent a few unhappy months in a church choir (my mum's idea, not mine). And two or three times a week, I had to sit through the sermon, delivered by an insufferable old windbag of a vicar. I thought it would last forever, and sometimes I thought it would kill me—that I would, quite literally, die of boredom. The only thing we were allowed for diversion was the hymnbook, and I even ended up reading it, sometimes. Books and comics had never seemed so necessary; even though I'd always enjoyed reading before then, I'd never understood it to be so desperately important for my sanity. I've never, ever gone anywhere without a book or a magazine since. It's taken me all this time to learn that it doesn't have to be a boring one, whatever the reviews pages and our cultural commentators tell me; and it took the Polysyllabic Spree, of all people, to teach me.

Please, please: put it down. You'll never finish it. Start something else. ✶

FEBRUARY 2005

BOOKS BOUGHT:
* *The Men Who Stare at Goats*—Jon Ronson
* *I Am Charlotte Simmons*—Tom Wolfe
* *Devil in the Details: Scenes from an Obsessive Girlhood*—Jennifer Traig
* *Palace Walk*—Naguib Mahfouz
* *Just Enough Liebling*—edited by David Remnick

BOOKS READ:
* *The Plot Against America*—Philip Roth
* *Father Joe: The Man Who Saved My Soul*—Tony Hendra
* *Chronicles: Volume One*—Bob Dylan
* *Little Children*—Tom Perrotta
* *Soldiers of Salamis*—Javier Cercas
* *The Book of Shadows*—Don Paterson

The story so far: I have been writing a column in this magazine for the last fifteen months. And though I have had frequent battles with the Polysyllabic Spree—the fifty-five disturbingly rapturous and rapturously disturbing young men and women who edit the *Believer*—I honestly thought that things had got better recently. We seemed to have come to some kind of understanding, a truce. True, we still have our differences of opinion: they have never really approved of me reading anything about sport, and nor do they like me referring to books wherein people eat meat or farmed fish. (There are a whole host of other rules too ridiculous to mention—for example, you try finding "novels which express no negative and/or strong emotion, either directly or indirectly"—but I won't go into them here.) Anyway, I was stupid enough to try to accommodate their whims, and you can't negotiate with moral terrorists. In my last column, I wrote a little about cricket, and I made a slightly off-color joke about Chekhov, and that was it: I was banned from the magazine, sine die, which is why my column was mysteriously absent from the last issue and replaced by a whole load of pictures. Pictures! This is how they announce my death! It's like a kind of happy-clappy North Korea round here.

I have no idea whether you'll ever get to read these words, but my plan is this: not all the fifty-five members of the Spree are equally sharp, frankly speaking, and they've got this pretty dozy woman on sentry duty down at the *Believer* presses. (Sweet girl, loves her books, but you wouldn't want her doing the Harold Bloom interview, if you know what I mean.) Anyway, we went out a couple of times, and I've told her that I've got the original, unedited, six-hundred-page manuscript of *Jonathan Livingston Seagull,* her favorite novel. I've also told her she can have it if she leaves me unsupervised for thirty minutes while I work out a way of getting "Stuff I've Been Reading" into the magazine. If you're reading these words, you'll know it all came off. This is guerrilla column-writing, man. We're in uncharted territory here.

They couldn't have picked a worse time to ban me, because I read my ass off last month. *Gravity's Rainbow, Daniel Deronda,* Barthes's *S/Z,* an enormous biography of some poet or another that was lying around… it was insane, what I got through. And it was all for nothing. This month I read what I wanted to read, rather than what I thought the Spree might want me to read, and there was nothing I wanted to read more than *Chronicles* and *The Plot Against America.*

I'm not a Dylanologist—to me he's your common-or-garden great artist, prone to the same peaks and troughs as anyone else and with nothing of any interest in his trash can. Even so, when I first heard about a forthcoming Dylan autobiography, I still found it hard to imagine what it would look like. Would it have a corny title— *My Back Pages*, say, or *The Times, They Have A-Changed*? Would it have photos with captions written by the author? You know the sort of thing: "The eyeliner years. What was *that* all about?!!?" Or, "Mary Tyler Moore and I, Malibu, 1973. Not many people know that our breakup inspired *Blood on the Tracks*." Would he come clean about who those Five Believers really were, and what was so obvious about them? Even if you don't have much time for the myth of Dylan, it's still hard to imagine that he'd ever be able to make himself prosaic enough to write autobiographical prose.

Chronicles ends up managing to inform without damaging the mystique, which is some feat. In fact, after reading the book, you end up realizing that Dylan isn't willfully obtuse or artful in any way—it's just who he is and how his mind works. And this realization in turn has the effect of contextualizing his genius—maybe even diminishing it, if you had a lot invested in his genius being the product of superhuman effort. He thinks in apocalyptic metaphors and ellipses, and clearly sees jokers and thieves and five (or more) believers everywhere he looks, so writing about them is, as far as he is concerned, no big deal. Here he is describing the difference a change in his technique made to him: "It was like parts of my psyche were being communicated to by angels. There was a big fire in the fireplace and the wind was making it roar. The veil had lifted. A tornado had come into the place at Christmastime, pushed all the fake Santa Clauses aside and swept away the rubble…." The boy can't help it. (My favorite little enigmatic moment comes when Dylan tells us how he arrived at his new surname, an anecdote that includes a reference to "unexpectedly" coming across a book of Dylan Thomas's poems. Where did the element of surprise come in, do you think? Did it land on his head? Did he find it under his pillow one morning?)

What's so impressive about *Chronicles* is the seriousness with which Dylan has approached the task of explaining what it's like to be him and how he got to be that way. He doesn't do that by telling you about his childhood or about the bath he was running when he started humming "Mr. Tambourine Man" to himself for the first time; *Chronicles* is nonlinear and concentrates on tiny moments in a momentous life—an afternoon in a friend's apartment in New York in 1961, a couple of days in New Orleans in 1989, recording *Oh Mercy* with Daniel Lanois. But he uses these moments like torches, to throw light backwards and forwards, and by the end of the book he has illuminated great swathes of his interior life—the very part one had no real hope of ever being able to see.

And *Chronicles* is a lot humbler than anyone might have anticipated, because it's about wolfing down other people's stuff as much as it's about spewing out your own. Here is a random selection of names taken from the second chapter: the Kingston Trio, Roy Orbison, George Jones, Greil Marcus, Tacitus, Pericles, Thucydides, Gogol, Dante, Ovid, Dickens, Rousseau, Faulkner, Leopardi, Freud, Pushkin, Robert Graves, Clausewitz, Balzac, Miles Davis, Dizzy Gillespie, Leadbelly, Judy Garland, Hank Williams, Woody Guthrie.... Many of the writers on this list were apparently encountered for the first time on a bookshelf in that NYC apartment. I have no idea whether the shelf, or the apartment, or even the friend actually existed, or whether it's all an extended metaphor; and nor do I care, because this is a beautiful, remarkable book, better than anyone had any right to expect, and one of the best and most scrupulous I can remember reading about the process of creativity. You don't even have to love the guy to get something out of it; you just have to love people who create any art at all.

For a brief moment, as I put down *Chronicles* and picked up *The Plot Against America,* neither of them published for longer than

a fortnight, I felt like some kind of mythical reader, dutifully plow-
ing through the "new and noteworthy" list. I knew almost enough
about what's *au courant* to throw one of those dinner parties that
the newspaper columnists in England are always sneering at.
They're invariably referred to as "Islington dinner parties" in the
English press, because that's where the "liberal intelligentsia"—aka
the "chattering classes"—are supposed to live, and where they talk
about the new Roth and eat focaccia, which is a type of bread that
the "chattering classes" really, really like, apparently. Well, I live in
Islington (there's no entrance exam, obviously), and I've never
been to a dinner party like that, and this could have been my
moment to start a salon. I could have bought that bread and said
to people, "Have you read the new Roth?" as they were taking off
their coats. And they'd have gone, like, "What the fuck?" if they
were my friends, or "Yes, isn't it marvelous?," if they were people
I didn't know. Anyway, it's too late now. The books have been out
for ages. It's too late for the dinner party, and it's too late even to
impress readers of this column. The Spree took care of that with
their pictures. This was the one chance I had to show off, and they
ruined it, like they ruin everything.

What's even more galling is that I had something to say about
The Plot Against America, and that almost never happens. The truest
and wisest words ever written about reviewing were spoken by
Sarah Vowell in her book *Take the Cannoli.* Asked by a magazine to
review a Tom Waits album, she concludes that she "quite likes the
ballads," and writes that down; now all she needs is another eight-
hundred-odd words restating this one blinding aperçu. That's pretty much how I feel about a lot of things I read and hear, so the
realization that I actually had a point to make about Roth's novel
came as something of a shock to me. You'll have heard my point a
million times by now, but tough—I don't have them often enough
to just let them float off.

Actually, if I put it this way, my point will have the virtue of novelty and freshness: in my humble and partial opinion, my brother-in-law's alternative-history novel *Fatherland* was more successful as a work of fiction. (You've never heard anyone say that, right? Because even if you've heard someone compare Roth's book to *Fatherland,* they won't have begun the sentence with "My brother-in-law…." My brother could have said it, but I'll bet you any money you like, he hasn't read the Roth. He probably lied about having read *Fatherland,* come to think of it.) *The Plot Against America* is a brilliant, brilliantly argued, and chilling thesis about America in the twentieth century, but I'm not sure it works as a novel, simply because one is constantly reminded that it is a novel—and not in a fun, postmodern way, but in a strange, slightly distracting way. As you will know, *The Plot Against America* is about what happened to the U.S. after the fascist-sympathizer Charles Lindbergh won the 1940 presidential election, but for large chunks of the book, this is *precisely* what it's about: the alternative history drives the narrative, and as a consequence, you find yourself wondering why we're being told these things. Because if Lindbergh became U.S. president in 1940—and this book asks us to believe that he did, asks us to inhabit a world wherein this was a part of our history—then surely we know it all already? Surely we know about the rampant anti-Semitism and the ensuing riots, the heroic role that Mayor LaGuardia played, and Lindbergh's eventual fate? We read on, of course, because we don't know, and we want to know; but it's an uncomfortable compulsion, working as it does against the novel's easy naturalism. When Roth writes, for example, that "the November election hadn't even been close… Lindbergh got 57 percent of the popular vote," the only thing the sentence is doing is providing us with information we don't have; yet at the same time, we are invited to imagine that we do have it—in which case, why are we being given it again?

In *Fatherland,* my brother-in-law—Harris, as I suppose I should call him here—takes the view that in an alternative-history novel, he must imagine not only the alternative history, but the historical consciousness of his reader; in other words, the alternative history belongs in the background, and the information we need to understand what has taken place (in *Fatherland,* the Nazis have won World War II) is given out piecemeal, obliquely, while the author gets on with his thriller plot. Roth chooses to place his what-if at the center of his book, and so *The Plot Against America* ends up feeling like an extended essay.

The thing is, I don't even know if I care. Did any of this really spoil my enjoyment of *The Plot Against America*? Answer: no. I could see it, but I didn't feel it. Who wouldn't want to read an extended essay by Philip Roth? It's only on the books pages of newspapers that perceived flaws of this kind inhibit enjoyment, and that's because book reviewers are not allowed to say "I quite like the ballads."

I now see that just about everything I read was relatively new: Tom Perrotta's absorbing and brave satire *Little Children,* Tony Hendra's mostly lovable *Father Joe….* *Soldiers of Salamis* is, I think, the first translated novel I've read since I began this column. Is that shameful? I suppose so, but once again, I don't feel it. When you're as ill-read as I am, routinely ignoring the literature of the entire non-English-speaking world seems like a minor infraction.

In Scottish poet Don Paterson's clever, funny, and maddeningly addictive new book of epigrams, *The Book of Shadows,* he writes that "nearly all translators of poetry… fail to understand the poem's incarnation in its tongue is *all there is of it,* as a painting is its paint." I suppose this can't be true for novels, but there is always the sense that you're missing something. *Soldiers of Salamis* is moving and informative and worthwhile and well translated and blah blah, and on just about every page I felt as though I were listening to a radio that hadn't quite been tuned in properly. You don't need to write in to express your disgust and disappointment. I'm disappointed enough in myself.

The Book of Shadows, though, came through loud and clear—FM through Linn speakers. Thought for the day: "Anal sex has one serious advantage: there are few cinematic precedents that instruct either party how they should *look*." Your bathroom needs this book badly. ★

MARCH 2005

BOOKS BOUGHT:
* *Case Histories*
  —Kate Atkinson
* *The Crocodile Bird*
  —Ruth Rendell
* *The Spy Who Came in from the Cold*—John le Carré
* *Another Bullshit Night in Suck City*—Nick Flynn
* *Help Us to Divorce*
  —Amos Oz

BOOKS READ:
* *Man on the Moon*
  —Simon Bartram
* *Every Secret Thing*
  —Laura Lippman
* *Help Us to Divorce*
  —Amos Oz
* *Assassination Vacation*
  —Sarah Vowell
* *Early Bird*
  —Rodney Rothman

So this last month was, as I believe you people say, a bust. I had high hopes for it, too; it was Christmastime in England, and I was intending to do a little holiday comfort reading—*David Copperfield* and a couple of John Buchan novels, say, while sipping an eggnog and... wait a minute! I only just read *David Copperfield*! What the hell's going on here?

Aha. I see what's happened. In hoping to save myself some time by copying out the sentence that began this column a year ago, I neglected to change anything at all. If I'd substituted *Barnaby Rudge* for *David Copperfield,* say, I might have got away with it, but I couldn't be bothered, and now I'm paying the price. A few months ago—back in the days when the Polysyllabic Spree used to tell me, repeatedly and cruelly, that they had commissioned research showing I had zero readers—I could have got away with repeating whole columns. But then, gloriously and unexpectedly, a reader wrote in ["Dear the *Believer*," November 2004] and the Spree had to eat their weasel words. My reader's name is Caroline, and she actually plowed through *Copperfield* at my suggestion, and I love her with all my heart. I think it's time to throw the question back at the Spree: so how many readers do you have, then?

Anyway, Caroline also responded to my recent plea for a list of thrillers that might make me walk into lampposts, which is how come I read Laura Lippman's *Every Secret Thing*. I really liked it, although at the risk of alienating my reader at a very early stage in our relationship, I have to say that it didn't make me walk into a lamppost. I'm not sure that it's intended to be that propulsive: it's gripping in a quiet, thoughtful way, and the motor it's powered with equips the author to putter around the inside of her characters' damaged minds rather than to smash her reader headlong into an inert object. On Lippman's thoughtful and engaging website—and there are two adjectives you don't see attached to that particular noun very often—a reviewer compares *Every Secret Thing* to a Patricia Highsmith novel, and the comparison made sense to me: like Lippman, Highsmith wants to mess with your head without actually fracturing your skull. *Every Secret Thing* is an American-cheeseburger version of Highsmith's bloody filet mignon, and that suited me fine.

Like many parents, I no longer have a lot of desire to read books in which children are harmed. My imagination is deficient and puny in every area except this one, where it works unstoppably for eighteen or twenty hours a day; I really don't need any help from no thriller. *Every Secret Thing* opens with the release from prison of two girls jailed for the death of a baby, and no sooner are they freed than another child disappears. "It's not incidental that a childless woman wrote *Every Secret Thing,* and I was *very* worried about how readers would react," Lippman said in an interview with the crime writer Jeff Abbott, but I suspect that it's precisely *because* Lippman is childless that she doesn't allow her novel to be pulled out of shape by the narrative events within it. I recently saw *Jaws* again, for the first time since it was in the cinema, and I'd forgotten that a small boy is one of the shark's first victims; what's striking about the movie now is that the boy is chomped and then pretty much forgotten about. In the last thirty years, we've sentimentalized kids and childhood to the extent that if *Jaws* were made now, it would have to be about the boy's death in some way, and it would be the shark that got forgotten about. *Every Secret Thing* is suitably grave in all the right places, but it's not hysterical, and it's also morally complicated in ways that one might not have expected: the mother who lost a child in the original crime is unattractively vengeful, for example, and it's her bitterness that is allowed to drive some of Lippman's narrative. My reader, huh? She shoots, she scores.

Assassination Vacation is the first of the inevitable *Incredibles* cash-ins—Sarah Vowell, as some of you may know, provided the voice of Violet Parr in *The Incredibles,* and has chosen to exploit the new part of her fame by writing a book about the murders of Presidents Lincoln, Garfield, and McKinley. See, I don't know how good an idea this is, from the cash-in angle. Obviously I'm over here in London, and I can't really judge the appetite for fascinating facts about the Garfield presidency among America's preteens, but I reckon Vowell might have done better with something more contemporary—a book about the Fair Deal, say, or an analysis of what actually happened at Yalta.

I should own up here and say that Sarah Vowell used to be a friend, back in the days when she still spoke to people who weren't sufficiently famous to warrant animation. She even knows some of the Spree, although obviously she's been cast out into the wilderness since she started bathing in asses' milk, etc. Anyway, I make a walk-on appearance in *Assassination Vacation*—I am, enigmatically, a smoker from London called Nick—and Vowell writes of the four hours we spent sitting on a bench in a cold Gramercy Park staring at a statue of John Wilkes Booth's brother. (This was her idea of a good time, not mine.)

Being reminded of that day made me realize how much I will miss her, because, incredibly, ha ha, she made those four hours actually interesting. Did you know that John Wilkes came from this prestigious acting family, a sort of nineteenth-century Baldwin clan? Hence the Booth Theatre in New York, and hence the statue in the park? There's loads more of this sort of stuff in *Assassination Vacation:* she trawls round museums examining bullets and brains and bits of Lincoln's skull, and hangs out in mausoleums, and generally tracks down all sorts of weird, and weirdly resonant, artifacts and anecdotes. If any other of my friends had told me that they were writing a book on this subject, I'd probably have moved house just so that they wouldn't have had a mailing address for the advance copy. But Vowell's mind is so singular, and her prose is so easy, and her instinct for what we might want to know so true, that I was actually looking forward to this book, and I wasn't disappointed. It's sad, because she does such a good job of bringing these people back to life before bumping them off again, and it's witty, of course (Garfield's assassin Charles Guiteau was a hoot, if you overlook the murderous bit), and, in the current political climate, it's oddly necessary—not least because it helps you to remember that all presidencies and all historical eras end. I hope her new friends, Angelina and Drew and Buzz and Woody and the rest, value Sarah Vowell as much as we all did.

Those of you who like to imagine that the literary world is a vast conspiracy run by a tiny yet elite cabal will not be surprised to learn that I read Rodney Rothman's book because Sarah recommended it, and she happened to have an advance copy because

Rothman is a friend of hers. So, to recap: a friend of mine who's just written a book which I read and loved and have written about gives me a book by a friend of hers which she loved, so I read it and then I write about it. See how it works? Oh, you've got no chance if you have no connection with One of Us. Tom Wolfe, Patricia Cornwell, Ian McEwan, Michael Frayn, Ann Rivers Siddons... You're doomed to poverty and obscurity, all of you. Anyway, Rothman's book is the story of how he went to live in a retirement community in Florida for a few months, and it's very sweet and very funny. If you're wondering why a man in his late twenties went to live in a retirement community in Florida, then I can provide alternative explanations. Rothman's explanation is that he wanted to practice being old, which is a good one; mine is that he had a terrific idea for a nonfiction book, which in some ways is even better, even if it's not the sort of thing you're allowed to own up to. Travel writers don't have to give some bullshit reason why they put on their kayaks and climb mountains—they do it because that's what they do, and the idea of voluntarily choosing to eat at 5 p.m. and play shuffleboard for half a year simply because there might be some good jokes in it is, I would argue, both heroic and entirely laudable.

In *Early Bird*, Rothman discovers that he's hopeless at both shuffleboard and bingo, and that it's perfectly possible to find septuagenarians sexually attractive. He gets his ass kicked at softball by a bunch of tough old geezers, and he tries to resuscitate the career of a smutty ninety-three-year-old stand-up comic with the catchphrase "But what the hell, my legs still spread." There are very few jokes about Alzheimer's and prune juice, and lots of stereotype-defying diversions. And Rothman allows the sadness that must, of course, attach itself to the end of our lives to seep through slowly, surely, and entirely without sentiment.

So this last month was, as I believe you people say... oh. Right. Sorry. What I'm trying to say here is that, once again, I didn't read as much as I'd hoped over the festive season, and one of the chief reasons for that was a book. This book is called *Man on the Moon*, and I bought it for my two-year-old son for Christmas, and I swear that I've read it to him fifty or sixty times over the last couple of weeks. Let's say that it's, what, two thousand words long? So that's 120,000-odd words—longer than the Alan Hollinghurst novel I still haven't read. And given I haven't got many other books to tell you about, I am reduced to discussing the salient points of this one, which has, after all, defined my reading month.

I bought *Man on the Moon* after reading a review of it in a newspaper. I don't normally read reviews of children's books, mostly because I can't be bothered, and because kids—my kids, anyway— are not interested in what the *Guardian* thinks they might enjoy. One of my two-year-old's favorite pieces of nighttime reading, for example, is the promotional flyer advertising the *Incredibles* that I was sent (I don't wish to show off, but I know one of the stars of the film personally), a flyer outlining some of the marketing plans for the film. If you end up having to read that out loud every night, you soon give up on the idea of seeking out improving literature sanctioned by the liberal broadsheets. I had a hunch, however, that what with the Buzz Lightyear obsession and the insistence on what he calls Buzz Rocket pajamas, he might enjoy a picture book about an astronaut who commutes to the moon every day to tidy it up. I dutifully sought the book out—and it wasn't easy to find, you know, just before Christmas—only to be repaid with a soul-crushing enthusiasm, when I would have infinitely preferred a polite, mild, and temporary interest. Needless to say, I won't be taking that sort of trouble again.

After his busy day on the moon, Bob the astronaut, we're told, has a nice hot bath, because working on the moon can make you pretty "grubby." And as my son doesn't know the word "grubby," I substitute the word "dirty," when I remember. Except I don't always remember, at which point he interrupts—somewhat tetchily—with

the exhortation "Do 'dirty'!" And I'll tell you, that's a pretty disconcerting phrase coming from the mouth of a two-year-old, especially
when it's aimed at his father. He says it to his mum, too, but I find
that more acceptable. She's a very attractive woman.

Amos Oz's *Help Us to Divorce* isn't really a book—it's two little essays published between tiny soft covers. But as you can see,
I'm desperate, so I have to include it here. Luckily, it's also completely brilliant: the first essay, "Between Right and Right," is a
clear-eyed, calm, bleakly optimistic view of the Palestinian crisis,
so sensible and yet so smart. "The Palestinians want the land they
call Palestine. They have very strong reasons to want it. The Israeli
Jews want exactly the same land for exactly the same reasons,
which provides for a perfect understanding between the parties,
and for a terrible tragedy," says Oz, in response to repeated invita-
tions from well-meaning bodies convinced that the whole conflict
could be solved if only the relevant parties got to know each other
better. I wanted Oz's pamphlet to provide me with quick and easy
mental nutrition at a distressingly mindless time of year; it worked
a treat. He kicked Bob the astronaut's ass right into orbit. ✶

A *selection from*

ASSASSINATION VACATION

by SARAH VOWELL

★ ★ ★

I live six blocks down Twenty-first Street from Gramercy Park and even though I walk by it every other day, I have been inside it precisely once, when my friend Nick, a Londoner, came to town and stayed at the Gramercy Park Hotel. How fitting that I cannot enter a park on my street without the escort of a subject of the British crown.

Nick gets the hotel's bellman to unlock the gate for us. Then the bellman asks how long we would like to stay. Why does he care? Because he has to know when to come back and *un*lock the gate. Unbelievable.

Nick seems to like the park, but then he likes anyplace in America where he can smoke. We mosey toward Edwin's behind. A life-size bronze in Elizabethan garb, his head's bowed, as if he's about to ask Hamlet's that-is-the-question question. Like the Prince of Denmark, Edwin could have come up with at least three reasons not to be. For starters, little brother going down in history as the president's killer was a cringing, galling shame. Before that, as a boy on the road with his drunken actor father, Junius Brutus Booth, when Edwin finally chose his own stage career over being Junius's babysitter, the elder Booth only lasted a few days without him, drinking rancid river water and dying, sick, on the Mississippi. Though it's hard to blame a kid for wanting more out of life than holding back his father's hair every night as he vomited up his Shakespearean pay, Edwin felt responsible for Junius's demise. Not that this guilt kept Edwin off the bottle. When Mary, his first and favorite wife, was lying on her deathbed in Boston, Edwin was in New York, too smashed to make the last train north. She was dead when he got there. He kicked himself for the rest of his life.

"So who was he?" Nick asks, pointing at Edwin's statue.

"Only the greatest Shakespearean actor of the nineteenth century."

Says the English accent, "You mean, in America?"

Whatever. I let that slide. I've been dying to get inside this park for years, but eventually, I'm going to need Nick and his bellman to get me out.

I tell him how Edwin was known as *the* Hamlet of his day; how his father, Junius Brutus was the greatest Shakespearean actor in England, until 1821, when he emigrated to Maryland, at which point he became the greatest Shakespearean actor in America; how three of Junius's children became actors themselves—Edwin, John Wilkes, and Junius Brutus Jr.; how the three brothers appeared onstage together only once, in *Julius Caesar* here in New York in 1864 as a benefit performance for the Shakespeare statue in Central Park; how their performance was interrupted because that was the night that Confederate terrorists set fires in hotels up and down Broadway and Edwin, who was playing Brutus, interrupted the play to reassure the audience; how the next morning Edwin informed John at breakfast that he had voted for Lincoln's reelection and they got into one of the arguments they were always having about North versus South; how Edwin retired from acting out of shame when he heard his brother was the president's assassin, but that nine months later, broke, he returned to the stage here in New York, as Hamlet, to a standing ovation; how he bought the house on Gramercy Park South and turned it into the Players Club, a social club for his fellow thespians and others, including Mark Twain and General Sherman; how he built his own theater, the Booth, on Twenty-third and Sixth, where Sarah Bernhardt made her American debut; and how, in the middle of the Civil War, on a train platform in Jersey City, he rescued a young man who had fallen onto the tracks and that man was Robert Todd Lincoln, the president's son, so he's the Booth who saved a Lincoln's life.

It is remarkable that Edwin earned back the public's affection after his brother had committed such a crime. It says something about his talent and his poise that he could pull this off. I have a recording of Edwin, performing Othello, from an 1890 wax cylinder. It sounds like a voice from the grave, so thick with static the only phrase I can understand is "little shall I." Though I cannot make out most of the words, something of Edwin's gentleness comes across, a kind of wispy melancholy I can imagine inspiring more sympathy than scorn.

Perhaps this is the approach Dr. Mudd's grandson Richard should have taken. Instead of spending his very long life pestering state legislatures to pass resolutions recognizing his grandfather's innocence, if he really wanted to get the country behind his family name, he should have recorded a hit song or come up with a dance craze or something.

In Bel Air, the Booths' hometown in Maryland, Edwin is a local hero. The Edwin Booth Memorial Fountain stands in front of the courthouse, next to a sign announcing that Edwin made his theatrical debut in the building. A WPA mural in the post office depicts the scene: a gangly teenager in tails leans pompously toward the assembled audience, half of whom have their heads in their hands they look so bored. A roadside historical marker at Tudor Hall reads, "The home of the noted actor Junius Brutus Booth, the Elder. Birthplace of his children. His son Edwin Booth was born here November 13, 1833." That's the whole sign. No mention of John Wilkes unless you count that cryptic reference to "his children."

Edwin's Players Club still exists in Gramercy Park. It remains the club Edwin envisioned, a fancy place for actors and their friends to get together. Edwin, the illegitimate son of a drunk, the heartbroken brother of an assassin, longed for propriety and ele gance. He was an actor back when the theater was one of the trashier professions. His actor brother offing the president in a theatre didn't improve his profession's profile. Thus did Edwin establish the Players. It's a beautiful house. I've been inside a few times, mostly for literary events. The last time I went, after wandering around and admiring the Edwin memorabilia on display—the John Singer Sargent portrait of Edwin hanging over the fireplace, the helmet he wore as Brutus in *Julius Caesar*—I listened to a novelist confess that his childhood sexual awakening occurred while watching a Porky Pig cartoon in which Porky dressed up in high heels.

Edwin would have loved his statue in Gramercy Park—the first statue of an actor in the city. He warranted a stained-glass window too—a multicolored Shakespearean portrait in the Church of the Transfiguration on Twenty-ninth. Known as the Little Church Around the Corner, it became an actors' church in the nineteenth century because it was the one church in town where actors would be granted a proper funeral.

The church hosted Edwin's funeral on June 9, 1893. Just as his pallbearers were carrying his coffin out the door in New York, in Washington, three floors of Ford's Theatre collapsed. The building had been turned into a government office building after the Lincoln assassination. Twenty-two federal employees died. ✶

APRIL 2005

BOOKS BOUGHT:
* *Saturday*—Ian McEwan
* *Towards the End of the Morning*—Michael Frayn
* *The 9/11 Commission Report*
* *How to Be Lost* —Amanda Eyre Ward
* *Katherine Mansfield: A Secret Life*—Claire Tomalin

BOOKS READ:
* *Saturday*—Ian McEwan
* *Towards the End of the Morning*—Michael Frayn
* *Case Histories* —Kate Atkinson
* *So Now Who Do We Vote For?*—John Harris
* *Another Bullshit Night in Suck City*—Nick Flynn

A few years ago, I was having my head shaved in a local barbers' when the guy doing the shaving turned to the young woman working next to him and said, "This bloke's famous."

I winced. This wasn't going to end well, I could tell. Any fame that you can achieve as an author isn't what most people regard as real fame, or even fake fame. It's not just that nobody recognizes you; most people have never heard of you, either. It's that anonymous sort of fame.

The young woman looked at me and shrugged.

"Yeah," said the barber. "He's a famous writer."

"Well, I've never heard of him," said the young woman.

NICK HORNBY

"I never even told you his name," said the barber.

The young woman shrugged again.

"Yeah, well," said the barber. "You've never heard of any writers, have you?"

The young woman blushed. I was dying. How long did it take to shave a head, anyway?

"Name one author. Name one author ever."

I didn't intercede on the poor girl's behalf because it didn't seem to be that hard a question, and I thought she'd come through. I was wrong. There was a long pause, and eventually she said, "Ednit."

"Ednit?" said her boss. "Ednit? Who the fuck's Ednit?"

"Well, what's her name, then?"

"Who?"

"Ednit."

Eventually, after another two or three excruciating minutes, we discovered that 'Ednit' was Enid Blyton, the enormously popular English children's author of the 1940s and 1950s. In other words, the young woman had been unable to name any writer in the history of the world—not Shakespeare, not Dickens, not even Michel Houellebecq. And she's not alone. A survey conducted by WHSmith in 2000 found that 43 percent of adults questioned were unable to name a favorite book, and 45 percent failed to come up with a favorite author. (This could be because those questioned were unable to decide between Roth and Bellow, but let's presume not.) Forty percent of Britons and 43 percent of Americans never read any books at all, of any kind. Over the past twenty years, the proportion of Americans aged 18–34 who read literature (and literature is defined as poems, plays, or narrative fiction) has fallen by 28 percent. The 18–34 age group, incidentally, used to be the one most likely to read a novel; it has now become the least likely.

And meanwhile, the world of books seems to be getting more bookish. Anita Brookner's new novel is about a novelist. David

Lodge and Colm Tóibín wrote novels about Henry James. In *The Line of Beauty,* Alan Hollinghurst wrote about a guy writing a thesis on Henry James. And in Ian McEwan's *Saturday,* the central character's father-in-law and daughter are both serious published poets and past winners of Oxford University's Newdigate Prize for undergraduate poetry. And though nobody should ever tell a writer what to write about…. Actually, forget that. Maybe somebody should. I have called for quotas in these pages before— I would have been great on some Politburo cultural committee— and I must call for them again. Nobody listens anyway. Sort it out, guys! You can't all write literature about literature! One book a year, maybe, between you—but all of the above titles were published in the last six months.

There are, I think, two reasons to be a little queasy about this trend. The first is, quite simply, that it excludes readers; the woman in the barbers' is not the only one who wouldn't want to read about the Newdigate Prize. And yes, maybe great art shouldn't be afraid of being elitist, but there's plenty of great art that isn't, and I don't want bright people who don't happen to have a degree in literature to give up on the contemporary novel; I want them to believe there's a point to it all, that fiction has a purpose visible to anyone capable of reading a book intended for grown-ups. Taken as a group, these novels seem to raise the white flag: we give in! It's hopeless! We don't know what those people out there want! Pull up the drawbridge!

And the second cause for concern is that writing exclusively about highly articulate people…. Well, isn't it cheating a little? McEwan's hero, Henry Perowne, the father and son-in-law of the poets, is a neurosurgeon, and his wife is a corporate lawyer; like many highly educated middle-class people, they have access to and a facility with language, a facility that enables them to speak very directly and lucidly about their lives (Perowne is "an habitual observer of his own moods"), and there's a sense in which McEwan is wasted on them. They don't need his help. What I've always loved about fiction is its ability to be smart about people who aren't themselves smart, or at least don't necessarily have the resources to describe their own emotional states. That was the way Twain was smart, and Dickens; and that is surely one of the reasons why Roddy Doyle is adored by all sorts of people, many of whom are infrequent book-buyers. It seems to me to be a more remarkable gift than the ability to let extremely literate people say extremely literate things.

It goes without saying that *Saturday* is a very good novel. It's humane and wise and gripping, just like *Atonement* and *Black Dogs* and just about everything McEwan has written. Set entirely on the day of the antiwar march in February 2003, it's about pretty much everything—family, uxoriousness, contemporary paranoia, the value of literature, liberalism, the workings of the human brain—and readers of this magazine will find much with which they identify. I spent too much time wondering about Henry Perowne's age, however. McEwan tells us that he's forty-eight years old, and though of course it's possible and plausible for a forty-eight-year-old man to have a daughter in her early twenties, it's by no means typical of highly qualified professional people who must have spent a good deal of their twenties studying; at the end of the book, (SKIP TO THE NEXT SENTENCE IF YOU DON'T WANT TO KNOW) Perowne learns that he is about to become a grandfather, and this too bucks a few demographic trends. I belong to Henry Perowne's generation, and my friends typically have kids who are now in their early-to-mid-teens. On top of that, I'm not sure that I am as consumed by thoughts of my own mortality as Perowne, although to be fair I'm a lot dimmer than he is, and as a consequence it may take me longer to get there. McEwan himself is fifty-six, and it felt to me like Perowne might have been, too. It doesn't matter much, of course, but the author's decision perhaps inevitably invites attempts at psychoanalysis.

It made me sad, thinking back to the day of the antiwar march.

All that hope! All that confidence! And now it's dwindled to nothing! I should explain that Arsenal beat Man Utd two–nil that afternoon in an FA Cup match—my passionate opposition to the war was conquered by my passionate desire to watch the TV—and it looked as though we would beat them forever. In fact, we haven't beaten them since, and I finished *Saturday* in the very week that they thumped us 4–2 at Highbury to end all championship aspirations for the season.

Usually, when I read a novel I'm enjoying, I just lie there with my mouth open, occasionally muttering things like "Oh, no! Don't go in there!" or "You could still get back together, right? You love each other." But both *Saturday* and Kate Atkinson's novel *Case Histories* contain detailed descriptions of places where I used to live and work, and as a consequence there were moments when I forgot to maintain even that level of critical engagement. Whenever Kate Atkinson mentioned Parkside, a street in Cambridge, I exclaimed—out loud, the first few dozen times, and internally thereafter—"Parkside!" (I used to teach at Parkside Community College, you see, so that was weird.) And then whenever Ian McEwan mentioned Warren Street, or the Indian restaurants on Cleveland Street, the same thing happened: "Ha! Warren Street!" Or, "Ha! The Indian restaurants!" And if someone was in the room with me while I was reading, I'd say, "This book's set around Warren Street! Where I used to live!" (It's not a residential area, you see, so that was weird, too.) It felt entirely right that I should read these books back-to-back, and then I was sent a copy of John Harris's *So Now Who Do We Vote For?*, and I felt for a moment as though certain books were stalking me or something. Until someone writes a book called *I Know Where You Put Your House Keys Last Night,* I can't imagine a title more perfectly designed to capture my attention.

I am sorry if the following lesson in U.K. politics is redundant, but I'm going to give it anyway: our Democrats are already in

office. We voted the right way in 1997, and we have had a Labour
government ever since, and at the time of writing it is absolutely
certain that we will have one for the next five years: there will be
an election some time in 2005, and Blair will walk it. As you may
have noticed, the only problem is that the Labour government
turned out not to be a Labour government at all. It's not just that
Blair helped to bomb Iraq; he's also introducing the profit motive
into our once glorious National Health Service and allowing
some pretty dodgy people to invest in the education of our children. Sir Peter Vardy, an evangelical Christian car-dealer, wants cre-
ationism taught alongside theories of evolution, and in return for
two million pounds per new school he can do pretty much whatever he wants. He already controls a couple of schools in the
North of England.

I waited for this government all my voting life, and Harris's
title perfectly captures the disillusionment of several generations of
people who thought that when the Tories went, all would be right
with the world. Disappointingly, Harris tells me that I should carry
on doing what I've been doing: my local MP (and we don't elect
leaders, just local representatives of political parties) has voted
against everything I would want him to vote against, so it seems
unfair to castigate him for Blair's crimes and misdemeanors.
I wanted to be told that the Liberal Democrats, our third party, or
the Greens, or the vaguely nutty Respect Coalition, were viable
alternatives, but they're not, so we're stuffed. *So Now Who Do We
Vote For?* is a useful and impassioned book nevertheless; it's a brave
book, too—nobody wants to write anything that will self-destruct
at a given point in its publication year, and I don't think he's going
to pick up many foreign sales, either. John Harris, we salute you.

Another Bullshit Night in Suck City wasn't one of the stalker
books, but after a couple of recommendations, I wanted to read it
anyway. Nick Flynn's dark, delirious memoir describes his father's
journey from employment, marriage, and a putative writing career

to vagrancy and alcoholism. (The ambition to write, incidentally, is never abandoned, which might give a few of us pause for thought.) Nick loses touch with his dad; lives, not entirely companionably, with a few demons of his own; and then ends up working in a homeless shelter. And guess who turns up? One image in *Another Bullshit Night in Suck City,* of a homeless man sitting in the street in an armchair, watching a TV he has managed to hook up to a street lamp, is reminiscent of Beckett; readers will find themselves grateful that Flynn is a real writer, stonily indifferent to the opportunities for shameless manipulation such an experience might provide.

I bought Michael Frayn's *Towards the End of the Morning* from one of Amazon's "Marketplace Sellers" for 25p. I could have had it for 1p, but I was, perhaps understandably, deterred rather than attracted by the price: what can you get for a penny these days? Would I be able to read it, or would all the pages have been masticated by the previous owner's dog? It wasn't as if I was entirely reassured by the higher price, but a few days later, a perfectly preserved, possibly unread 1970 paperback turned up in the post, sent by a lady in Scotland. Does anyone understand this Marketplace thing? Why does anyone want to sell a book for a penny? Or even twenty-five pennies? What's in it for anyone, apart from us? I'm still suspicious. It's a wonderful novel, though, urbane and funny and disarmingly gentle, and I might send the lady in Scotland some more money anyway. Or is that the scam? That's clever.

"If Frayn is about to step into anybody's shoes, they aren't Evelyn Waugh's but Gogol's," says the blurb on the front of my thirty-five-year-old paperback. Is that how you sold books back then? And how would it have worked? As far as I can work out, the quote is a stern warning to fans of elegant English comic writing that this elegant English comic novel won't interest them in the slightest. It was a daring tactic, certainly; the penny copies lead one to suspect that it didn't quite come off. ✶

MAY 2005

BOOKS BOUGHT:

* *Sleep Toward Heaven*
  —Amanda Eyre Ward
* *Dr. Seuss: American Icon*
  —Philip Nel

BOOKS READ:

* *In Cold Blood*
  —Truman Capote
* *A Cold Case*
  —Philip Gourevitch
* *Like A Rolling Stone*
  —Greil Marcus
* *How to Be Lost*
  —Amanda Eyre Ward

Earlier today I was in a bookstore, and I picked up a new book about the migration patterns of the peregrine falcon. For a moment, I ached to buy it—or rather, I ached to be the kind of person who would buy it, read it, and learn something from it. I mean, obviously I could have bought it, but I could also have taken the fifteen pounds from my pocket and eaten it, right in the middle of Borders, and there seemed just as much point in the latter course of action as the former. (And before anyone gets on at me about Borders, I should point out that the last independent bookshop in Islington, home of the chattering literary classes, closed down a couple of weeks ago.)

I don't know what it was about, the peregrine falcon thing. That's some kind of bird, right? Well, I've only read one book about a bird before, Barry Hines's heartbreaking *A Kestrel for a Knave,* later retitled *Kes* to tie in with Ken Loach's film adaptation of that name. (You, dear reader, are much more likely to have read *Jonathan Livingston Seagull* than *Kes,* I suspect, and our respective tastes in bird books reveal something fundamental about our cultures. An Amazon reviewer describes *Jonathan Livingston Seagull* as "a charming allegory with a very pertinent message: DON'T ABANDON YOUR DREAMS." I would not be traducing the message of *Kes* if I were to summarize it thus: ABANDON YOUR DREAMS. In fact, "ABANDON YOUR DREAMS" is a pretty handy summary of the whole of contemporary English culture—of the country itself, even. It would be great to be you, sometimes. I mean, obviously our motto is more truthful than yours, and ultimately more useful, but there used to be great piles of *Kes* in every high school stockroom. You'd think they'd let us reach the age of sixteen or so before telling us that life is shit. I read Hines's book because it was a work of literature, however, not because it was a book about a bird. And maybe this book will turn out to be a work of literature, too, and a million people will tell me to read it, and it will win tons of prizes, and eventually I'll succumb, but by then, it will have lost the allure it seemed to have this afternoon when it promised to be the kind of book I don't usually open. I'm always reading works of bloody literature; I'm never reading about migration patterns.

This month, my taste in books seems to have soured on me: every book I pick up seems to be exactly the sort of book I always pick up. On the way home from the bookstore, as I was pondering the unexpectedly seductive lure of the peregrine falcon, I tried to name the book least likely to appeal to me that I have actually read all the way through, and I was struggling for an answer. Isn't that ridiculous? You'd have thought that there'd been something, somewhere—an apparently ill-advised dalliance with a book about mathematics or physics, say, or a history of some country that I didn't know anything about, but there's nothing. I read a biography of Margaret Thatcher's press secretary once, but my brother-in-law wrote it, so that doesn't really count. And I did struggle through Roy Jenkins's enormous *Gladstone,* which reduced me to tears of boredom on several occasions, but that was because I was judging a nonfiction prize. I would like my personal reading map to resemble a map of the British Empire circa 1900; I'd like people to look at it and think, *How the hell did he end up right over there?* As it is, I make only tiny little incursions into the territory of my own ignorance—every year, another classic novel conquered here, a couple of new literary biographies beaten down there. To be honest, I'm not sure that I can spare the troops for conquests further afield: they're needed to quell all the rebellions and escape attempts at home. But that's not the attitude. When you turn to these pages next month, I swear you'll be reading about peregrine falcons, or Robert the Bruce, or the combustion engine. I'm sorry that the four books I read these last few weeks seem to have brought all this on, because I loved them all. But look at them: a cute, sad literary novel, a couple of elegant true-crime stories, and a book about Dylan by one of America's cleverest cultural commentators—chips off the old block, every one of them. I can hardly claim to have pushed back any personal frontiers with any of these.

Recently the Polysyllabic Spree, the fifteen horrifically enthusiastic young men and women who control the minds of everyone who writes for this magazine, sent an emissary to London, and the young man in question handed me, without explanation, a copy of Philip Gourevitch's *A Cold Case.* I felt duty-bound to read it, not least because the Spree frequently chooses enigmatic methods of communication, and I presumed that the book would contain some kind of coded message. In fact, the purpose of the gift was straightforwardly cruel: the security tag was still attached to it, and as a consequence I was humiliated by store detectives whenever I tried to enter a shop with the book in my bag. I don't really know why the Spree wanted to do this to me. I suspect it's something to do with the recent discovery that I have one reader (a charming and extremely intelligent woman called Caroline—see the March issue) whereas there is still no evidence that they have any at all. I've tried not to be triumphalist, but even so, they haven't reacted with great magnanimity, I'm afraid.

A Cold Case is a short, simple, and engrossing account of a detective's attempt to solve a twenty-seven-year-old double homicide—or rather, to find out whether the prime suspect is still alive. The detective's renewed interest in the case seems almost alarmingly whimsical (he happens to drive past a bar which reminds him of the night in question), but his rigor and probity are unquestionable, and one of the joys of the book is that its characters—upright, determined detective, psychotic but undeniably magnetic villain—seem to refer back to the older, simpler, and more dangerous New York City. In one of my favorite passages, Gourevitch reports verbatim the conversations he overhears in the office of a colorful lawyer with a lot of Italian-American clients:

> [*Enter Rocco, a burly man with a voice like a cement mixer*]
> RICHMAN:Your father and I grew up together... Your mother is a beautiful lady.
> ROCCO: She sure is...
> RICHMAN:Your uncle—the first time I had him, he was thirteen years old.
> ROCCO:Yup.
> RICHMAN: I represented Nicole when she killed her mother, when she cut her mother's throat.
> ROCCO:Yes, yes, I remember that.

The end of this exchange raises the alarming possibility of an alternate version, wherein Rocco had forgotten all about Nicole cutting her mother's throat. And though I do not wish to generalize about the people or person who reads this magazine, I'm sure I speak for all of us when I say that we would have retained at least the vaguest memory of an equivalent occasion in our own lives.

I was shamed into reading *In Cold Blood* at one of Violet Incredible's London literary soirees. I think I may have mentioned before that I know Violet Incredible of *The Incredibles* personally. Anyway, ever since the success of that film, she has taken to gathering groups of writers around her, presumably in the hope that she becomes more literary (and, let's face it, less animated) by osmosis. I don't know why we all turn out. I suppose the truth is that we are none of us as immune to the tawdry glitter of Hollywood as we like to pretend. At the most recent of these events, most of the writers present suddenly started enthusing about Truman Capote's 1965 nonfiction classic. And though it goes without saying that I joined in, for fear of incurring Violet's disapproval, I've never actually read the thing.

It makes a lot of sense reading it immediately after *A Cold Case,* and not just because they belong in the same genre. Philip Gourevitch thanks David Remnick in his acknowledgments, and Truman Capote thanks William Shawn; this is *New Yorker* true crime, then and now (ish), and the comparison is instructive. Capote's book is much wordier, and researched almost to within an inch of its life, to the extent that one becomes acutely aware of the information that is being concealed from the reader. (If he knows *this* much, you keep thinking, then he must know the rest, too. And of course anyone constructing a narrative out of real events knows more than they're letting on, but it's not helpful to be reminded so forcefully of the writer's omniscience.) Gourevitch's book is short, understated, selective. And though *A Cold Case* doesn't quite attain the heights that *In Cold Blood* reaches in

its bravura, vertiginously tense, unbearably ominous opening sec
tion, Gourevitch clearly reaps the benefits of Capote's ground-
breaking work. *In Cold Blood* is one of the most influential books
of the last fifty years, and as far as I can tell, just about every work
of novelistic nonfiction published since the 1960s owes it something or another. But the trouble with influential books is that if
you have absorbed the influence without ever reading the original, then it can sometimes be hard to appreciate the magnitude of
its achievement. I loved *In Cold Blood,* but at the same time I could
feel it slipping away from me as a Major Literary Experience—*A
Cold Case* seemed to me simultaneously less ambitious and more
sure-footed. I mean, I'm sure my impression is, you know, *wrong.*
But what can I do?

I read Amanda Eyre Ward's lovely *How to Be Lost* after a warm
recommendation from a friend, and it's got the mucus, as P. G.
Wodehouse would and did say. ("The mucus" was to Wodehouse's
way of thinking a desirable attribute, lest people think this is some
kind of snotty snark.) *How to Be Lost* isn't one of those irritating-
ly perfect novels that people sometimes write; it has a slightly
ungainly, gawky shape to it, and slightly more plot than it can swallow without giving itself heartburn. But it has that lovely tone that
only American women writers seem to be able to achieve: melan-
cholic, wry, apparently (but only apparently) artless, perched on the
balls of its feet and ready to jump either toward humor or toward
heartbreak, with no run-up and no effort. *How to Be Lost* has a
great setup, too. Narrator Caroline, a New Orleans barmaid with
a drinking habit, has/had a sister who disappeared without a trace
when she was a little girl. Just as Caroline's family is about to
declare Ellie dead, Caroline spots a photo in a magazine of a
woman in a crowd whose face contains an unmistakable trace of
the child she knew, and she sets off to track the woman down.
Good, no?

How to Be Lost is about all the usual stuff you read in literary novels: grief and families and disappointment and so on, and I was interested in what Ward had to say about all of these things. But as far as I was concerned, she'd earned the right to sound off because she'd lured me into her book with an intriguing narrative idea. It doesn't hurt, that's all I'm saying. The Kate Atkinson novel I read a few weeks back had a longtime absent little sister in it, too. But where *Case Histories* (and Atkinson is English) differs from *How to Be Lost* is…. Are you going to read either of these? Perhaps you will. Well, remember the bird books, and choose accordingly.

The last book I read that contained the wealth and range of cultural references on show in Greil Marcus's *Like a Rolling Stone* was Bob Dylan's *Chronicles.* Those of you who've read Dylan's breathtakingly good memoir might remember that one of the many, many names (of writers, artists, historians, musicians) in there was that of Marcus himself, and there is no reason why Marcus shouldn't have helped Dylan to think about culture in the same way that he's helped many of us think about culture.

For the second time this month I found myself envying the advantages that being an American can bring, although on this occasion I envied only those who live and think in America; you can't envy those who live in America and don't think (although you could argue that those who don't think aren't really living anyway). One of the things that Marcus's book is about is the slipperiness of meaning in the U.S.; any major American artist, in any idiom, can change the way the country perceives itself. I'm not sure this is possible here in England, where our culture appears so monolithic, and our mouthiest cultural critics so insanely and maddeningly sure of what has value and what doesn't. If we have never produced a Dylan, it is partly because he would have been patronized back into obscurity: we know what art is, pal, and it's nothing you'd ever have heard on Top 40 radio. I didn't always understand *Like a Rolling Stone* (and I can't for the life of me hear the things that Marcus can in the Pet Shop Boys' version of "Go West"), but my sporadic bafflement didn't matter to me in the least. Just to live in the world of this book, a world of intellectual excitement and curiosity and rocket-fueled enthusiasm, was a treat.

STOP PRESS: Since I began this column, a friend has had an idea for a literary genre I'd never touch in a million years: SF/Fantasy, of the nonliterary, nerdy-boys-on-websites variety. He's right, and already my heart is sinking in a gratifying way. Do I have to? I'm already wishing I'd shelled out for the peregrine falcon book. ✴

JUNE/JULY 2005

BOOKS BOUGHT:
* *Little Scarlet*—Walter Mosley
* *Out of the Silent Planet*
  —C. S. Lewis*
* *Voyage to Venus*—C. S. Lewis*
* *Maxton*—Gordon Brown*
* *Nelson and His Captains*
  —Ludovic Kennedy*
* *Excession*—Iain M. Banks

BOOKS READ:
* *Excession*—Iain M. Banks
  (abandoned)
* *The Men Who Stare at*
  Goats—Jon Ronson
* *Adrian Mole and the Weapons*
  of Mass Destruction
  —Sue Townsend
* *The Wonder Spot*
  —Melissa Bank
* *Stuart: A Life Backwards*
  —Alexander Masters

The story so far: suddenly sick of my taste in books, I vowed in these pages last month to read something I wouldn't normally pick up. After much deliberation (and the bulk of the otherwise inexplicable Books Bought can be explained by this brief but actually rather exhilarating period), I decided that my friend Harry was right, and that in the normal course of events I'd never read an SF/Fantasy novel in a million years. Now read on, if you can be bothered.

Even buying Iain M. Banks's *Excession* was excruciating. Queu-

---

*Don't worry. These books were bought for one pound or less at the Friends of Kenwood House Book Sale.

ing up behind me at the cash desk was a very attractive young woman clutching some kind of groovy art magazine, and I felt obscurely compelled to tell her that the reason I was buying this purple book with a spacecraft on the cover was because of the *Believer,* and the *Believer* was every bit as groovy as her art magazine. In a rare moment of maturity, however, I resisted the compulsion. She could, I decided, think whatever the hell she wanted. It wasn't a relationship that was ever going to go anywhere anyway. I'm with someone, she's probably with someone, she was twenty-five years younger than me, and—let's face it—the *Believer* isn't as groovy as all that. If we had got together, that would have been only the first of many disappointing discoveries she'd make.

When I actually tried to read *Excession,* embarrassment was swiftly replaced by trauma. Iain M. Banks is a highly rated Scottish novelist who has written twenty-odd novels, half of them (the non-SF half) under the name Iain Banks, and though I'd never previously read him, everyone I know who is familiar with his work loves him. And nothing in the twenty-odd pages I managed of *Excession* was in any way bad; it's just that I didn't understand a word. I didn't even understand the blurb on the back of the book: "Two and a half millennia ago, the artifact appeared in a remote corner of space, beside a trillion-year-old dying sun from a different universe. It was a perfect black-body sphere, and it did nothing. Then it disappeared. Now it is back." This is clearly intended to entice us into the novel—that's what blurbs do, right? But this blurb just made me scared. An arti-fact—that's something you normally find in a museum, isn't it? Well, what's a museum exhibit doing floating around in space? So what if it did nothing? What are museum exhibits supposed to do? And this dying sun—how come it's switched universes? Can dying suns do that?

The urge to weep tears of frustration was already upon me even before I read the short prologue, which seemed to describe some kind of androgynous avatar visiting a woman who has been pregnant for forty years and who lives on her own in the tower of a giant spaceship. (Is this the artifact? Or the dying sun? Can a dying sun be a spaceship? Probably.) By the time I got to the first chapter, which is entitled "Outside Context Problem" and begins "(*GCU Grey Area* signal sequence file #n428857/119)," I was crying so hard that I could no longer see the page in front of my face, at which point I abandoned the entire ill-conceived experiment altogether. I haven't felt so stupid since I stopped attending physics lessons aged fourteen. "It's not *stupidity*," my friend Harry said when I told him I'd had to pack it in. "Think of all the heavy metal fans who devour this stuff. You think you're dimmer than them?" I know that he was being rhetorical, but the answer is: yes, I do. In fact, I'm now pretty sure that I've never really liked metal because I don't understand that properly, either. Maybe that's where I should start. I'll listen to Slayer or someone for a few years, until I've grasped what they're saying, and then I'll have another go at SF. In the meantime, I have come to terms with myself and my limitations, and the books I love have never seemed more attractive to me. Look at them: smart and funny novels, nonfiction books about military intelligence and homeless people…. It's a balanced, healthy diet. I wasn't short of any vitamins. I was looking for the literary equivalent of grilled kangaroo, or chocolate-covered ants, not spinach, and as I am never drawn to the kangaroo section of a menu in a restaurant, it's hardly surprising that I couldn't swallow it in book form.

Stupidity has been the theme of the month. There's a lot of it in Jon Ronson's mind-boggling book about U.S. military intelligence, *The Men Who Stare at Goats;* plenty of people (although admittedly none of us is likely to spend much time with) would describe the behavior of the tragic and berserk Stuart in Alexander Masters's brilliant book as stupid beyond belief. And Sue Townsend's comic anti-hero Adrian Mole, who by his own admission isn't too bright, has unwittingly contributed to the post-*Excession* debate I've been having with myself about my own intelligence.

Adrian Mole is one of the many cultural phenomena that has passed me by until now, but my friend Harry—yes, the same one, and no, I don't have any other friends, thank you for asking—suddenly declared Townsend's creation to be a work of comic genius, and insisted I should read *Adrian Mole and the Weapons of Mass Destruction* immediately. He pointed out helpfully that I'd understand quite a lot of it, too, and as I needed the boost in confidence, I decided to take his advice.

Adrian Mole, who famously began his fictional life aged thirteen and three-quarters, is now thirty-four, penniless, becalmed in an antiquarian bookshop, and devoted to our Prime Minister. One of the many unexpected pleasures of this book was the acerbity of its satire. There is real anger in here, particularly about the war in Iraq, and the way Townsend manages to accommodate her dismay within the tight confines of light comedy is a sort of object lesson in what can be done with mainstream fiction. There's a great running gag about Blair's ludicrous claim that Saddam could hit Cyprus with some of the nasty missiles at his disposal: Adrian Mole has booked a holiday on that very island, and spends much of the book trying to reclaim his deposit from the travel agent.

I do wish that comic writing took itself more seriously, though. I don't mean I want fewer jokes; I simply mean that the cumulative effect of those jokes would be funnier if they helped maintain the internal logic of the book. Mole has a blind friend, Nigel, to whom he reads books and newspapers, and at one point Nigel accuses him of not understanding much of what he's reading. "I had to admit that I didn't," Mole says, before, just a few pages later, making an admittedly inappropriate allusion to Antony Beevor's *Stalingrad*. It might seem pedantic to point out that anyone who's plowed their way through *Stalingrad* is probably capable of grasping the essence of a newspaper article (if not the opening of an Iain M. Banks novel)—just as it's probably literal-minded to wonder how an unattractive man with a spectacularly unenviable romantic history gets repeatedly lucky with an extremely attractive woman. But moments like this tend to wobble the character around a little bit, and I found myself having occasionally to recreate him in my head, almost from scratch. I'm sure that Mole has a fixed identity for those who have read the entire series, and he remains a fantastic, and fantastically English, comic creation: upright and self-righteous, bewildered, snobby, self-hating, provincial, and peculiarly lovable. We all are, here.

Jon Ronson's *The Men Who Stare at Goats* is one of the most disorienting books I have ever read. While reading it, I started feeling like the victim of one of the extremely peculiar mindfuck experiments that Ronson describes in his inimitable perplexed tones. Here's his thesis: after the rout in Vietnam, the U.S. military started investigating different ways to fight wars, and as a consequence co-opted several somewhat eccentric New Age thinkers and practitioners who, your generals felt, might point them toward a weaponless future, one full of warriors capable of neutralizing the enemy with a single glance. And the first half of the book is uproarious, as Ronson endeavors to discover, for example, whether the actress Kristy McNichol (who appeared in *The Love Boat II* and the cheesy soft porn movie *Two Moon Junction*), had ever been called upon to help find Manuel Noriega. (A U.S. Sergeant called Lyn Buchanan, who was part of a secret unit engaged in a "supernatural war" against Noriega, had repeatedly written her name down while in a self-induced trance, and became convinced that the actress knew something.) Gradually Ronson builds a crazy-paving path that leads to Abu Ghraib, and both the book and its characters become darker and more disturbing.

You have probably read those stories of how people in Iraq and Afghanistan were tortured by having American pop music blasted at them day and night. And you have probably read or heard many of the jokes made as a consequence of these stories—people writing in to newspapers to say that if you have a teenager who listens to 50 Cent or Slipknot all day then you know how those Iraqi prisoners feel, etc. and so on. (Even the *Guardian* made lots of musical torture jokes for a while.) Ronson floats the intriguing notion that the jokes were an integral part of the strategy: in other words, if you can induce your citizens to laugh at torture, then outrage will be much harder to muster. Stupidity is, despite all appearances to the contrary, a complicated state of mind. Who's stupid, in the end—them or us?

This month's Book by a Friend was Melissa Bank's *The Wonder Spot,* and this paragraph must be parenthetical, because neither the novel nor the friend can be shoehorned into the stupid theme. It's been a long time since *The Girls' Guide to Hunting and Fishing,* and some of us—including the author herself—were wondering whether she'd ever get around to a second book. But she has, finally, and it's a lovely thing, sweet-natured, witty, lots of texture. It's hard to write, as Bank does here, about growing up, and about contemporary adult urban romance: it's such an apparently overpopulated corner of our world that she must have been tempted, at least for a moment, by artifacts and dying suns and women who are pregnant for decades. We need someone who's really, really good at that stuff, though, because it still matters to us, no matter how many millions of words are written on the subject. In fact—and once again in these pages I'm calling for Soviet-style intervention into the world of literature—it would be much easier for everyone if Melissa Bank and maybe two or three other people in the world were given an official government license, and you could no more appoint yourself as chronicler of contemporary adult urban romance than you could set yourself up as a neurosurgeon. In this utopia, Melissa Bank would be… well, you'll have to insert the name of your own top neurosurgeon here. I don't know any. Obviously. I'm too dim. Damn that Iain M. Banks. He's wrecked my confidence.

Here's an unlikely new subgenre: biographical studies of vagrants. Alexander Masters's *Stuart: A Life Backwards* is, after *Another Bullshit Night in Suck City,* the second one I've read recently, and if these two are as successful as they should be, then on top of everything else, down-and-outs may have to contend with the unwanted attentions of hungry nonfiction writers. At the moment, there's still plenty of room in the field for tonal contrast; where Nick Flynn's book about his homeless, alcoholic father was poetic, as deep and dark and languid as a river, *Stuart* is quick, bright, angry, funny, and sarcastic—Masters finds himself occasionally frustrated by Stuart's inexplicable and self-destructive urge to punch, stab, self-lacerate, incinerate, and cause general mayhem. ("I headbutted the bloke," Stuart explains when Masters asks him what happened to a particular employer and job. "Excellent. Of course you did. Just the thing," Masters finds himself thinking.)

The story is told backwards at Stuart's suggestion, after he'd told Masters that his first draft was "bollocks boring"; he thinks the narrative structure will pep it up a little, turn it into something "like what Tom Clancy writes." It feels instead like a doomed search for hope and innocence; as Masters trudges back through three decades of illness and drug abuse and alcohol abuse and self-abuse and the shocking, sickening abuse perpetrated by Stuart's teachers and family members, he and we come to see that there never was any. This is an important and original book, and it doesn't even feel as though you should read it. You'll want to, however much good it's doing you.

I'm certain that I read five books all the way through in the last month, and yet I've written about only four of them. This means that I've forgotten about the other one completely, the first time that's happened since I began writing this column. I'm sorry, whoever you are, but I think you've got to take some of the blame.

Your book was... well, it was good, obviously, because we are forced by the Polysyllabic Spree, the sixty-three white-robed literary maniacs who run this magazine, to describe every book as good. But clearly it could have been better. Try a joke next time, or maybe a plot. ⭑

AUGUST 2005

BOOKS BOUGHT:

* *Gilead*
  —Marilynne Robinson
* *The Bullfighter Checks Her Makeup*—Susan Orlean
* *Housekeeping*—Marilynne Robinson*
* *You Are Here: Personal Geographies and Other Maps of the Imagination*
  —Katherine Harmon
* *Babbitt*—Sinclair Lewis
* *Between Silk and Cyanide*
  —Leo Marks
* *Bartleby the Scrivener*
  —Herman Melville
* *The Disappointment Artist*
  —Jonathan Lethem

* *Wonderland*
  —Michael Bamberger

BOOKS READ:

* *Gilead*
  —Marilynne Robinson
* *Little Scarlet*
  —Walter Mosley
* *Noblesse Oblige*
  —Nancy Mitford
* *Spies*—Michael Frayn
* *The Amateur Marriage*
  —Anne Tyler
* *Penguin Special*
  —Jeremy Lewis
* *Hard News*—Seth Mnookin
* *Jane Austen*—Gill Hornby

A few months ago, I heard a pompous twit on a radio program objecting, bitterly and at some length, to Martin Amis's *Money* being republished in the Penguin Modern Classic series. It couldn't possibly be a classic, said the pompous twit, because we need fifty years to judge whether a book is a classic or not. It seemed to me that the twit's argument could be summarized succinctly thus: "I don't like Martin Amis's *Money* very much," because nothing else made much sense. (Presumably we're not allowed to use the phrase "modern classic" about anything at

---

* *Bought twice—administrative error.*

all unless we wish to appear oxymoronic, even though in this context the word "classic" means, simply, "of the highest class." The pompous twit seemed to be laboring under the misapprehension that a "classic" book is somehow related to classical music, and therefore has to be a bit old and a bit posh before it qualifies.) Do you have Penguin Modern Classics in your country? Over here, they used to mean a lot to young and pretentious lovers of literature. My friends and I used to make sure we had a PMC, with its distinctive light green spine, about our persons at all times, as an indication both of our intellectual seriousness and of our desire/willingness to sleep with girls who also liked books. It never worked, of course, but we lived in hope. Anyway, *L'Étranger* was a Penguin Modern Classic; I probably read it in 1974, thirty-odd years after it was published. And when I was talking embarrassing rubbish about Sartre to fellow seventeen-year-olds, *La Nausée*— another light green 'un—had been around for less than forty years. If the pompous twit's fifty-year rule had been enforced when I was a teenager, I'd never have read either of them—we needed that green spine for validation—and as a consequence I'd be even more ill-educated than I am now.

Anyway, Marilynne Robinson's *Gilead* is clearly a modern classic, and it hasn't even been in print for five minutes. It's a beautiful, rich, unforgettable work of high seriousness, and you don't need to know that the book has already won the Pulitzer Prize to see that Robinson isn't messing around. I didn't even mind that it's essentially a book about Christianity, narrated by a Christian; in fact, for the first time I understood the point of Christianity—or at least, I understood how it might be used to assist thought. I am an atheist living in a godless country (7 percent of us attend church on a regular basis), so the version of Christianity I am exposed to most frequently is the evangelical U.S. version. We are a broad church here at the *Believer,* and I don't wish to alienate any of our subscribers who believe that gays will burn in hell for all eternity and so on, but your far-right evangelism has never struck me as being terribly conducive to thought—rather the opposite, if anything. I had to reread passages from *Gilead* several times—beautiful, luminous passages about grace, and debt, and baptism—before I half-understood them, however: there are complicated and striking ideas on every single page.

Gilead is narrated by a dying pastor, the Reverend John Ames, and takes the form of a long letter to his young son; the agony of impending loss informs every word of the book, although this agony has been distilled into a kind of wide-eyed and scrupulously unsentimental wonder at the beauty of the world. It's true that the book contains very little in the way of forward momentum, and one reads it rather as one might read a collection of poetry; it's only two hundred and fifty pages long, but it took me weeks to get through. (I kept worrying, in fact, about reading *Gilead* in the wrong way. I didn't want it to go by in dribs and drabs, but it seemed equally inappropriate to scoff something containing this amount of calories down in a few gulps.) This column has frequently suggested that a novel without forward momentum isn't really worth bothering with, but that theory, like so many others, turned out not to be worth the (admittedly very expensive) paper it was printed on: *Gilead* has turned me into a wiser and better person. In fact, I am writing these words in a theological college somewhere in England, where I will spend the next several years. I'll miss my kids, my partner, and my football team, but when God comes knocking, you don't shut the door in His face, do you? All this only goes to show that you never know how a novel's going to affect you.

We all of us know that the circumstances surrounding the reading of a book are probably every bit as important as the book itself, and I read *Gilead* at a weird time. I was on book tour in the U.K., and I was sick of myself and of the sound of my own voice, and of appearing on daft radio shows, where I found that it was surprisingly easy to reduce my own intricately wrought novel to idiotic sound bites: if anyone were ever in need of the astonishing hush that Marilynne Robinson achieves in her book—how do you do that, in something crafted out of words?—it was I. Caveat emptor, but if you don't like it, then you have no soul.

So *Gilead* is one of the most striking novels I have ever read, and it won the Pulitzer Prize, and it's a modern classic, but it doesn't win the coveted "Stuff I've Been Reading" book-of-the-month award. It didn't even come close, incredibly. That honor goes to my sister Gill's *Jane Austen: The Girl with the Magic Pen,* a biography intended for children but strongly recommended to anyone of any age. If you want me to be definitive about it, then I would say that whereas *Gilead* is one of the best new novels I've read for years, Hornby's biography is undoubtedly the best book of all time. Strong words, I know, but: it's ninety pages long! It's about Jane Austen, who was great, right? I rest my case.

My sister's work is, however, quite clearly, underneath it all, both about and aimed at me. Listen to this: "Jane's eldest brother, James, was busy trotting out lofty verse, in a manner befitting the vicar he was soon to become....There was no doubt, they all said, who was the writer in the family—and James readily (and a little smugly) agreed!" I think we can all read the subtext here, can't we? James Austen = NH. Jane Austen = GH. (Weirdly, my sister didn't even know about my recent decision to become a man of the cloth when she wrote those lines.) And what about this? "Families are funny things, and often cannot see what is under their noses." Hey, no need to beat around the bush! Just come out and say what's on your mind, Oh Great One! As if Mum ever allowed me to forget that you were the really clever member of the family. As if Mum didn't always love you more than me anyway.... Sorry. This probably isn't the most appropriate forum in which to air grievances of this kind, however justifiable. And in any case, if you're too dim to understand the book properly, to see it for what it really is—namely, a rage-fueled, ninety-page poison-pen letter to the author's brother—you'll find much to enjoy on the superficial level. She had to pretend at least that she was writing about Austen, and that stuff is great, lively, and informative. See? If I can be generous about your work, how come you can't bring yourself to.... Sorry again. I'm just going out for a cigarette and a walk. I'll be right back.

A whole bunch of these books I read for work. You can't just go on the radio and say, "Buy my new novel. It's great." Oh, no. That's not how it works. You have to go on the radio and say, "Buy *his* new novel. It's great." And then, according to the publicity departments at my publishers, the listening public is so seduced by the sound of your voice that it ignores what you're actually telling them, and goes out to buy your book anyway. We have this show called *A Good Read,* on which a couple of guests talk with the show's presenter about a book they love, and I chose Michael Frayn's *Spies,* which is a wonderful, complicated, simple novel about childhood, suburbia, and the Second World War. My fellow guest chose Nancy Mitford's *Noblesse Oblige,* which was published in the 1950s, and discusses the upper classes and their use of language—they say "lavatory," we say "toilet," that kind of thing. My fellow guest wasn't so keen on *Spies,* which was kind of hilarious, considering that he'd just made us plough through all this stuff about "napkin" versus "serviette." I won't say any more about *Noblesse Oblige,* as otherwise the Polysyllabic Spree will ban me for yet another issue, and I'm spending more time out than in as it is.

Our host, meanwhile, chose Anne Tyler's *The Amateur Marriage,* and both the choice and the novel itself made me very happy. Anne Tyler is the person who first made me want to write: I picked up *Dinner at the Homesick Restaurant* in a bookshop, started to read it there and then, bought it, took it home, finished it, and suddenly I had an ambition, for about the first time in my life. I was worried that *The Amateur Marriage* was going to be a little schematic: Tyler tells the story of a relationship over the decades, and the early part of the book is perhaps too tidy. In the '50s, the couple are living out America's postwar suburban dream, in the '60s they're on the receiving end of the countercultural revolution, and so on. But the cumulative details of the marriage eventually sprawl all over the novel's straight, tight lines as if Tyler were creating a garden; as it turns out, in those first chapters, she's saying, "Just wait for spring—I know what I'm doing." And she does, of course. Before too long, *The Amateur Marriage* is teeming with life and artfully created mess, and when it's all over, you mourn both the passing of Tyler's creation and the approaching end of her characters' lives.

My ongoing disciplinary troubles with the Polysyllabic Spree, the four hundred and thirty white-robed and utterly psychotic young men and women who control both the *Believer* and the minds of everyone who contributes to it, mean that I have to cram two months' worth of reading into one column. (I no longer have any sense of where I'm going wrong, by the way. I've given up. I think I may have passed on some admittedly baseless gossip about the Gawain poet at the monthly editorial conference, and it didn't go down well, but who knows, really?) So, in brief: Jeremy Lewis's biography of Allen Lane, the founder of Penguin, is a tremendous piece of social history, which I have already written about in *Time Out*. (It was the same deal as with *Spies*—I recommend someone else's book, this time in print, and everyone rushes out to buy mine. See how it works? You've got to hand it to the people who think this stuff up.) And Walter Mosley's *Little Scarlet* comprehensively rubbishes yet another theory this column has previously and unwisely expounded—that crime novels in a series are always inferior to what I believe the trade calls "stand-alones." Easy Rawlins is one of probably scores of exceptions to the rule, possibly because one of Mosley's aims in the Rawlins books is to write about race in twentieth-century America. *Little Scarlet* is set in L.A. during the Watts riots of 1965, and you never get the sense that you're whiling away the time; the stakes are high, and both detective and book demonstrate a moral seriousness that you don't find in many literary novels, never mind generic thrillers.

Seth Mnookin is yet another member of Violet Incredible's literary set. So those of us who pretend we still know her since she went all Hollywood animated have dutifully read his book about Jayson Blair and the *New York Times,* even though the subject has nothing to do with us, for fear that we'll be cast into the darkness, far away from the warm glow of celebrity. Luckily, Mnookin's book is completely riveting: I doubt I'll read much else about U.S. newspaper culture, so it's just as well that this one is definitive. Mnookin's thoroughness—he explains with clarity and rigor how Blair and the *NYT* was an accident waiting to happen—could have resulted in desiccation, but it's actually pretty juicy in all the right places. None of the outrage Blair caused makes much sense to us in England—you can make up whatever you want here, and you'll never hear from a fact-checker or even an editor—so reading *Hard News* was like reading an Austen novel. You have to understand the context, the parameters of decency in an alien environment, to make any sense of it.

So I'm off on a book tour of the U.S. now, and I'm thinking of taking *Barnaby Rudge* with me. It'll last me the entire three weeks, and it's about the Gordon riots, apparently. I'll bet you can't wait for the next column. ✻

SEPTEMBER 2005

BOOKS BOUGHT:

* *The Diary of a Country
  Priest*—Georges Bernanos
* *A Complicated Kindness*
  —Miriam Toews
* *Blood Done Sign My Name*
  —Timothy B. Tyson
* *Over Tumbled Graves*
  —Jess Walter
* *Becoming Strangers*
  —Louise Dean

BOOKS READ:

* *Citizen Vince*—Jess Walter
* *A Complicated Kindness*
  —Miriam Toews

O n my recent book tour of the U.S. I met a suspiciously large number of people who claimed to be *Believer* readers; some of the people who came to the signings even told me that they had read and enjoyed this column, although I can see that if you're standing in front of someone waiting for a signature, you might as well say something, even if what you end up saying is patently and laughably untrue. Anyway, having met and talked to some of you, I now realize that the descriptions I occasionally provide of the Polysyllabic Spree, the eighty horribly brainwashed young men and women who control this magazine (and who may in turn, I am beginning to realize, be controlled by someone else), have been misleading. There are some misconceptions out there, and I feel it's only fair, both to you and to the Spree, to clear a few things up.

Numbers. The Spree consists of sixty-four people. You can safely ignore any other figure you may come across, either here or in the national media. Sometimes I have inflated or deflated the numbers, for comic purposes—because the joke of saying, for example, forty or eighty when really it's sixty-four is always funny, right? Or it could have been funny, if people weren't so literal-minded. My recent conversations have left me with the feeling that this particular witticism, along with several others (see below), may have fallen flat.

Robes. The trademark, telltale Spree white robes are only worn in certain circumstances, namely during editorial meetings, major sporting events (as a protest against their existence) and morning "prayers," wherein the Spree shout out the names of literary figures. (I can't tell you how disconcerting it is to hear otherwise attractive and frequently naked young women yelling out "SYBILLE BEDFORD!" in a banshee wail.) I'm sorry if I have somehow given the impression that they wear white robes all the time. They don't. In fact, given the propensity for nudity up at Believer Towers, I wish they'd put them on more often.

Free copies of the _Believer._ A while back I remarked in passing that I didn't ever see this magazine because the Spree refused to send me free copies. I can't say too much about this, because, sadly, it's all _sub judice,_ and my lawyers have told me to be careful about how I address the matter in print. In brief: I have discovered that the magazine and its new publishing venture is not, as I had been assured previously, a vanity publishing outfit, and that therefore I should not have been paying the company to have my columns and my book _The Polysyllabic Spree_ published. In a desperate attempt to avoid having their asses sued off, the Spree have started lavishing subscriptions and T-shirts upon me. It won't do them any good. Things have gone too far.

Suspensions. Similarly, I have in the past complained bitterly about my suspension from these pages after having ignored one of the Spree's many unfathomable and apparently random edicts. The truth is that I haven't been suspended by the Spree nearly as often as I've claimed; I made some of those stories up, usually to excuse my own indolence and/or temporary disappearances, usually prompted by the investigations of the relentless Child Support Agency here in the U.K.

I hope that's cleared a few things up and we can now all make a fresh start.

As you were probably beginning to suspect, the preceding nonsense was a crude attempt to deflect attention away from the dismal brevity of this month's "Books Read" list: for the first time since I began writing for this magazine, I have completely lost my appetite for books. I have half-read several, and intend to finish all of them, but at the moment I find it impossible to concentrate on what anyone has to say about more or less any subject. This seems, in part, to be something to do with my book tour—it's unfair, I know, but I seem to be sick of the sound of everyone's voice, not just my own. Plus, at the time of this writing, I live in a city which seems to be exploding about our ears, and this has done nothing at all for my interest in contemporary literature. It all seems a bit beside the point at the moment. I'm sure that's an error in my thinking, and that my unwillingness to engage with sensitive first novels about coming out on a sheep farm in North Dakota in the 1950s—I made this book up, by the way, and if you wrote it, I mean no offense—proves that the terrorists have won, to use the phrase that seems to end every sentence here at the moment. ("It means they've won" is applied indiscriminately to anyone's failure to do anything at all that they usually do. If you don't feel like getting on a tube or a bus, going into the center of the city, reading a book, getting drunk, or punching someone on the nose, it means you're a scaredy-cat, not British, etc.) Instead of reading, I play endless games of solitaire on my mobile phone, watch twenty-four-hour news channels, and try to find newspaper articles written by experts on fundamentalism assuring me that this will all be over by Tuesday. I haven't found any such reassurance yet. This morning I found myself moderately uplifted by a piece in the *Times* explaining that acetone peroxide, the explosive that London bombers favor, has a shelf life of less than a week. It's cheap, though, and available in any half-decent hardware store, so it's not all good news.

Anyway, in this context it seems something of a miracle that I've finished any books at all. Jess Walter, a wonderful writer of whose existence I was previously unaware, sent me *Citizen Vince* in the hope that I might start a third list at the top of this page, a list entitled "Books Foisted upon Me," so I was immediately intrigued by his novel; as a freelance reviewer I get sent a ton of books, but nobody to date has expressed an ambition to appear in a *Believer* list. If I hadn't actually gone and read the thing I might have been tempted.

The clincher for me was an enthusiastic blurb by the great Richard Russo, and he didn't let me down, because *Citizen Vince* is fast, tough, thoughtful, and funny. (Right at the beginning of the book there's a terrific scene involving an unwilling hooker and her unsatisfied customer, a scene culminating in an interesting philosophical debate about whether there's such a thing as half a blow job.) It's about a guy who's moved from New York City to Spokane, Washington, under the Witness Protection Program; he's going about his business of making doughnuts and committing petty fraud when it becomes apparent that a man who may or may not be connected to Vince's past wants to kill him. And this guy, the bad guy, he's really, *really* bad. He threatens to do something so vile to a small child that you can't read on until you've started breathing again.

Citizen Vince would have worked fine as "just" a thriller, but

Walter has ambitions on top of that, because it's also about voting, believe it or not; Vince has been registered by the authorities, and for the first time in his life he has to decide who he wants as president. The book's set in 1980, so the choice is between Carter and Reagan, and Vince is paralyzed by it; this is hardly surprising, seeing as Walter suggests that the choice is between the America you ended up with, and another America, one that vanished when poor, decent, hopeless Jimmy was beaten. In a couple of bravura passages, Walter leaves his gangsters and petty crooks to fend for themselves while he enters the minds of the candidates themselves. I loved this novel. It came through my letter box just when I was beginning to think that I'd have to write "NONE!" under the heading "Books Read"; it seemed to know that what I needed was pace, warmth, humor, and an artfully disguised attempt to write about a world bigger than the one its characters live in.

Miriam Toews's lovely *A Complicated Kindness* is funny, too, but it's not overly bothered about pace, not least because it's partly about the torpor that comes from feeling defeated. Last month, I believe I threatened to get religion; I may even have said that I'd gone to live in a monastery, but before anyone at a reading asks me how I'm enjoying the monastic life, I should explain that this was another of those jokes where I say that something is so when it is in fact not so. (Maybe it's a cultural thing, these jokes falling flat? But then again, I don't make anyone laugh here either.) Anyway, *A Complicated Kindness* has further delayed my plans to turn my back on this vale of tears: Nomi Nickel, Miriam Toews's narrator, is a Mennonite, or at least she comes from a family of Mennonites, and she doesn't make it sound like too much fun.

Mennonites—and everyone's a Mennonite where Nomi lives—are against the things that make life bearable: sex, drugs, rock and roll, makeup, TV, smoking, and so on; Nomi Nickel, on the other hand, is for all of those things, wherein lies both the tension and the torpor. Nomi's sister Tash and her mother have already been driven out of town by the Mennonite powers-that-be, but Nomi has stayed behind to look after her father, Ray, a man who spends a lot of time sitting on his lawn chair and staring into space; Nomi, meanwhile, bounces round the town off the diamond-hard disapproval she meets everywhere, getting into all the trouble she can, which isn't so much, in a town that doesn't even have a bus station—it was removed because the more rebellious spirits kept wanting to go places. One of the joys of the book, in fact, is the desperate ingenuity of its characters, looking for ways to express themselves in a culture that allows no self-expression. "That was around the time our Aunt Gonad asked Tash to burn her *Jesus Christ Superstar* soundtrack. Tash could do a hilariously sexy version of 'I Don't Know How to Love Him' where she basically worked herself into a complete fake orgasm during that big crescendo." You may think that you don't want to read about the problems of being brought up Mennonite, but the great thing about books is that you'll read anything that a good writer wants you to read. And the voice that Miriam Toews finds for her narrator is so true and so charming that you don't even mind spending a couple hundred pages in a town as joyless as Nomi's East Village.

I bought *A Complicated Kindness* in the Powell's bookstall at the Portland, Oregon, airport, after several fervent recommendations from the Powell's staff who looked after me at my signing. Did you know that you have the best bookshops in the world? I hope so. Over here in England, the home of literature ha-ha, we have only chain bookstores, staffed by people who for the most part come across as though they'd rather be selling anything else anywhere else; meanwhile you have access to booksellers who would regard their failure to sell you novels about Mennonites as a cause of deep personal shame. Please spend every last penny you have on books from independent bookstores, because otherwise you'll end up as sour and as semi-literate as the English.

I bought *The Diary of a Country Priest* in a fit of post-*Gilead* enthusiasm, although I have to say that at the moment, my chances of reading it, at least in this life, are slim. I was tempted, however, by the following review on the Amazon site:

> *This book has had an enormous impact on my life. Having had to read it as part of my French A level course (in French!) it left me psychologically scarred. Grinding through each passage was like torture, making me weep with frustration and leaving me with a long-burning and deep-felt resentment against my French teacher and the A level exam board. This resulted in a low grade for my French lit paper, which offset a decent language paper, resulting in a 'C' which wasn't good enough for my chosen university. So I had to switch from French to business studies, so changing the course of my life. To say I detest this book is an understatement.*

You see the profound effect that literature can have on a life? Who says it's all a waste of time? If only I could produce one book that left someone with that kind of ferocious grievance. If you have read one of my books, you probably feel cheated out of however much money it might have cost you, and you'll certainly begrudge the time you wasted on it. But even at my most bullish and self-aggrandizing, I can't quite make myself believe that I've actually wrecked someone's life. Any documentary evidence to the contrary will be gratefully received. ✲

A *selection from*

CITIZEN VINCE

by JESS WALTER

★ ★ ★

Eighty-seven bars in greater Spokane, serving three hundred thousand people. One taxicab company: eight cabs. So on a Tuesday morning just past two a.m., last call, the economics are clear: more drunks than the market can bear. They leach out onto the sidewalks and stagger and yawn to their cars—those who own them and remember where they're parked. The rest walk from downtown to the neighborhoods, scattering in all directions across bridges, though underpasses, beneath trestles, up hills to dark residential streets, solitary figures beneath thought bubbles of warm breath and cigarette smoke. Rehearsed lies.

Vince Camden concentrates on his own thoughts as he walks sober and rested among the drunk and tired. Stout downtown brick and brownstone give way to low-rent low-rise strips— karate dojos, waterbed liquidators, erotic bookstores, pawnshops, and Asian massage—then a neighborhood of empty warehouses, rail lines, vacant fields, and a solitary two-story Victorian house, an after-hours cards and rib joint called Sam's Pit. This is where Vince hangs out most nights before his shift begins at the donut shop.

Vince was only in town a few months when Sam died. Thirty-seven. The new owner is named Eddie, but everyone calls him Sam—it being easier to change one's name to Sam than to change the faded Pepsi sign on the old house from SAM'S to EDDIE'S. Just as old Sam did, new Sam opens the Pit when the rest of the city closes, after Last Call. The place works like a drain for the city; every morning when the bars close, the drunks and hookers and lawyers and johns and addicts and thieves and cops and cardplayers—as old Sam used to say, "Evergodambody"—swirls around the streets and ends up here. It's why the cops don't sweat the gambling and undercounter booze. It's just nice to know that at three a.m., everyone will be gathered in one place, like the suspects in a seamy British drawing room.

The Pit lurks behind high, unkempt shrubs, the only thing on a block of vacant lots, like a last tooth. Behind, a rutted dirt field functions as a parking lot for Sam's and a factory showroom for the half-dozen professional women who gather here each night for last tricks. Inside, pimps play cards and wait for their cut.

Gravel cracks beneath Vince's shoes as he angles for Sam's Pit. Six cars are parked randomly in his weed-covered field, girls doing business in a couple. A car door opens fifty feet from Vince, and a woman's voice skitters across the weedy lot: "Let go!"

Vince stares straight ahead. *Not your business.*

"Vince! Tell this guy to let go of me!"

Beth's voice. At the door, Vince turns and walks back across the lot toward a tan Plymouth Duster. Inside, Beth Sherman is wrestling with a guy in a white turtleneck sweater and a navy sport coat. As he walks up to the car, Vince can see the guy's pants are open and that he's trying to keep Beth from getting out of the car. She swings at him with the frayed, dirty cast on her right forearm. Barely misses.

Vince leans down and opens the car door. "Hey, Beth. What's going on?"

The guy lets go and she pulls away, climbs out of the car and past Vince. He is amazed again how pretty she can be, triangular face and round eyes, bangs cut straight across them. She can't weigh a hundred pounds. Odd for a woman in her line of work to actually look younger than she is, but Beth could pass for a teenager—at least from a distance. Up close—well, the lifestyle is tough to hide. Beth points at the guy in the car with her cast. "He grabbed my ass."

The guy is incredulous. "You're a hooker!"

"I'm in real estate!"

"You were blowing me!"

Beth yells around Vince at the man: "Do you grab your plumber's ass when *he's* working?"

Vince steps between Beth and the john, and smiles disarmingly at the guy. "Look, she doesn't like to be touched."

"What kind of hooker doesn't like to be touched?"

Vince can't argue the premise. But he wishes the guy had just kept his mouth shut. He knows how this will go now, and in fact Beth steps around him, fishes around in her pocket, and throws a twenty-dollar bill in his face.

The guy holds up the twenty. "I gave you forty!"

"You got half," she says. "You get half your money back."

"Half? There's no such thing!" He looks up at Vince. "Is there such thing as half?"

Vince looks from Beth to the guy and opens his mouth without the slightest expectation that anything will come. He looks back at Beth and their eyes catch long enough for both of them to note.

About Beth Sherman: she is thirty-three, just leaving "cute," with brown hair and eyes that dart from attention. Her dislike of contact notwithstanding, Beth is well respected among the working women at Sam's, mostly for one big accomplishment—she quit heroin without methadone, cold fucking turkey, exactly nineteen months and two weeks ago, on the very day she found out she was pregnant. Her boy, Kenyon, is a little more than a year now and he seems fine, but everyone knows how she watches him breathlessly, constantly comparing him to the other kids in the park and at his day care, looking for any sign that he is slow or stunted, that her worst fears are realized, that the junk has ruined him, too. And while she is clearly on her way out of this life—she fired her pimp, *in writing*—Beth continues to turn tricks, maybe because there are so few ways for a high school dropout to support herself and her son. Anyway, she's not the only hooker at Sam's who introduces herself as something else. It's a place full of actresses and massage therapists, models, students, and social workers, but when Beth says she's in real estate, people actually seem to believe it.

When he first arrived, Vince purchased Beth's services (he tried a few of the girls) and found himself intrigued by her cool distance, the way she bristled under his hands. Then one night six months ago, she and Vince drank two bottles of wine and spent a night together *without* the exchange of money. And it was different—alarming and close. No bristle. But since then everything has been out of sorts—Beth not wanting to charge him, Vince wary of becoming involved with a woman with a kid. And so they haven't slept together in three months. The worst part is that it feels like cheating to be with the other women, and so Vince is in the midst of his longest stretch of celibacy that doesn't involve a jail cell. The whole thing has proven to him the old axiom among the professional class: *Free sex ruins everything.*

In the parking lot, Beth stalks away from the angry, unsated john—her tight jeans beneath a coat that stops midriff. Vince watches her go, then takes one of the bags of dope from his pocket, bends down, and holds it up to the window. The Bible says that even the peacemaker deserves a profit. Or it says something anyway.

After a second, the guy shrugs and holds up the twenty. "Yeah, okay," he says. As they exchange dope for money, the guy shakes his head. "Never heard of a hooker who didn't want to be touched."

Vince nods, although in his estimation the world is made of only such people, pot-smoking cops, thieves who tithe 10 percent, society women who wear garters, tramps who sleep with stuffed bears, criminal donut makers, real estate hookers. He remembers a firefighter in the old neighborhood named Alvin Dunphy who was claustrophobic. Died when a burning apartment building collapsed on him. Thirty-eight. ★

OCTOBER 2005

BOOKS BOUGHT:

None.

BOOKS READ:

★ *Blood Done Sign My Name*
—Timothy B. Tyson
★ *Candide*—Voltaire
★ *Oh the Glory of It All*
—Sean Wilsey

I want to take back some things I said last month. Or rather, I don't so much want to take them back as to modify my tone, which is a pretty poor show, considering that writing, especially writing a column, is all about tone: what I'm essentially saying is, don't read last month's column, because it was all wrong. I was way too defensive, I see now, about my relative lack of literary consumption (two books, for the benefit of those of you who are too busy busy busy to retain the minutiae of my reading life from one month to the next). Shamefully—oh, God, it's all coming back to me now—I tried to blame it on all sorts of things, including the London bombs, but the truth is that two books in a month isn't so bad. There are lots of people who don't get through two books a month. And anyway, what would happen if I had read no books? Obviously, I'd lose this job (although that's assuming one of the Spree noticed). But apart from that? What would happen if I read no books ever? Let's imagine someone who reads no books ever but polishes off every word of the *New Yorker,* the *Economist,* and their broadsheet newspaper of choice: well, this imaginary person would do more reading than me, because that's got to be a couple of hundred thousand words a week, and would also be a lot smarter than me, if you use that rather limited definition of smart which involves knowing stuff about stuff. The *New Yorker* has humor in it and also provides an introduction to contemporary fiction and poetry. So the only major food group not covered is starch: in other words, the classics. And what would happen if we never read the classics? There comes a point in life, it seems to me, where you have to decide whether you're a Person of Letters or merely someone who loves books, and I'm beginning to see that the book lovers have more fun. Persons of Letters have to read things like *Candide* or they're a few letters short of the whole alphabet; book lovers, meanwhile, can read whatever they fancy.

I picked up *Candide* because my publishers sent me a cute new edition, and though that in itself wouldn't have persuaded me, I flicked through it and discovered it was only ninety pages long. Ninety pages! Who knew, apart from all of you, and everybody else? A ninety-page classic is the Holy Grail of this column, and when the Holy Grail is pushed through your letter box, you don't put it on a shelf to gather dust. (Or maybe that's exactly what you'd do with the Holy Grail. Is it ornamental? Has anyone ever seen it?) Anyway, I have now read *Candide.* That's another one chalked off. And boy, does Voltaire really have it in for Leibnizian philosophy! Whoo-hoo! Now, there's a justification for reading *Candide* right there. Many of you will have been living, like Leibniz, in the deluded belief that all is for the best, in the best of all possible worlds (because you believe that God would have created nothing but the best), but I have read Voltaire, and I can now see that this is a preposterous notion that brings only despair. And it's not only Leibniz who comes in for a kicking, either. Oh, no. Corneille, the Jesuits, Racine, the Abbé Gauchat, Rousseau…. Just about everyone you've ever wanted to see lampooned in a short novel gets what's coming to them. You lot are probably all familiar with the Abbé Gauchat, the Theatines, the Jansenists, and the literary criticism of Élie-Catherine Fréron, but I'm afraid I found myself flicking frantically between the text and the footnotes at the end; I was unhappily reminded of the time I had to spend at school reading Alexander Pope's equally mordant attacks on poetasters and so forth. Literary types will tell you that underneath all the contemporary references, you will recognize yourselves and your world, but it's not true, of course. If it's this world you're after, the one we actually live in, you're better off with Irvine Welsh or Thomas Harris.

The trouble with *Candide* is that it's one of those books that we've all read, whether we've read it or not (cf. *Animal Farm, 1984, Gulliver's Travels, Lord of the Flies*). The meat was picked off it and thrown to the crowd in the eighteenth century, and… I'll abandon this metaphor here, because I suspect that it must inevitably conclude with digestive systems and the consumption of ancient excrement. The point is that we are familiar with silly old Dr. Pangloss, just as we know that some animals are more equal than others. Satires and allegories tend to have been decoded long before we ever get to them, which renders them somewhat redundant, it seems to me. *Panglossian* is the sort of word you might find from time to time in the *Economist* and the *New Yorker,* and in any case, if ever anyone lived in an age that had no need for a savage debunking of optimism, it is us. We believe that everything everywhere is awful, all the time. In fact, Voltaire was one of the people who first pointed it out, and he was so successful that we find ourselves in desperate need of a Pangloss in our lives. Bitter footnote: just after I'd finished my cute hardback, I found an old paperback copy on my shelves (unread, obviously): a hundred and thirty pages. Oh, the pain! I'd never have read—or paid, as you have to think of it in this case—three figures. I was tricked, swindled and cheated by my own publishers, who clearly scrunched everything up a bit to dupe the innocent and the ill read.

Book length, like time, is an abstract concept. Sean Wilsey's *Oh the Glory of It All* is a good four times the length of *Candide,* and I enjoyed it probably four times as much, even though all book logic suggests that the reverse might have been the case. I'm sure young Sean would be the first to admit that there's some sag around the middle, but like many of us, it's lovable even at its saggiest point. And also, you never once have to laugh at the pomposities of the French Academies of the eighteenth century, a prerequisite, I now understand, for any book. (In fact, publishers should use that as a blurb. "You never once have to laugh at the pomposities of the French Academies of the eighteenth century!" I'd buy any book that had that on the cover.)

Oh the Glory of It All is a memoir, as those of you who live in the Bay Area may already know; Wilsey was brought up in San Francisco by squillionaire socialites, although after his parents' divorce, the silver spoon wasn't as much use as he might have hoped: his mother devoted her time to saving the world, and dragged Sean off around the world to meet the Pope and various scary old-school Kremlin types; meanwhile his dad married a scary old-school stepmother who treated Wilsey like dirt. (Hey, Dede! You may be a bigshot in a little bit of San Francisco, but nobody has ever heard of you here in London! Or anywhere else! I'm sorry, but she got me so steamed up that I had to get back at her somehow.) He got chucked out of every school he attended, and ran away from a creepy establishment that didn't allow you to utter the names of rock bands out loud.

American lives seem, from this distance at least, very different from European lives. Look at this: Sean Wilsey's mother was the daughter of an itinerant preacher. She ran away to Dallas to be a model, an escape funded initially by the nickels from her uncle's jukeboxes and peanut machines. She was dragged off to California by her angry family, and while waitressing there she met a U.S. Air Force major who married her on a live national radio program called *The Bride and Groom*. She split from the major, dated Frank Sinatra for a while, married a couple of other guys—one marriage lasted six months; the other, to the trial lawyer who defended Jack Ruby, lasted three weeks. She got a TV job and she had a fan club. And then she married Sean's dad. We don't do any of that here. We don't have itinerant preachers, or peanut machines, or Sinatra. We are born in, for example, Basingstoke, and then we either stay there or we move to London. That's probably why we don't write many memoirs.

Timothy B. Tyson's *Blood Done Sign My Name* is a memoir, too, although it's not the peculiarities of his life that Tyson is writing about, but the point at which his experiences intersect with recent American history. Tyson was brought up in Oxford, North Carolina, where his father was the pastor of the Methodist church; in 1970, Robert Teel, the father of one of Tyson's friends, and a couple of other white thugs murdered a young black man, and after the contemptible trial, wherein everyone was found not guilty of everything, there was a race riot, and great chunks of Oxford got torched. Young Tim Tyson grew up to be a professor of Afro-American studies, and *Blood Done Sign My Name* is a perfect reflection of who he is now and where he came from: it's both memoir and social history, and it's riveting. Tyson has a deceptively folksy prose style that leads you to suspect that his book will in part be about the triumph of Civil Rights hope over bitter Southern experience, but it ends with a coda, a visit to a club in Greensboro, North Carolina, in 1992 to see Percy Sledge: Tyson's black friend is denied admission. Yes, 1992. Yes, Percy Sledge, the soul singer.

Blood Done Sign My Name is uncompromisingly tough minded, righteous, and instructive (there is a terrific section unraveling the taboo that surrounded black men sleeping with white women), and it's not about people singing "We Shall Overcome" and holding hands until blacks and whites live together in perfect harmony. On the contrary, Tyson is very good on how the history of the Civil Rights movement is being rewritten daily until it begins to look like the triumph of liberal good sense over prejudice; nothing would have happened, he argues, without things being set on fire. "If you want to read only one book to understand the uniquely American struggle for racial equality and the swirls of emotion around it, this is it," says one of the reviews on the back of the book. Well, I have read only one book about the uniquely American struggle for racial equality, and this was it. But I will read another one one day soon: it would seem strange, and perhaps a little perverse, to allow a white man to provide my entire Civil Rights education. I mean no offense to the author of this memorable book, but he'd be the first to admit that Afro-Americans might have something of interest to say on the subject.

I moved house this month and have bought no books at all for the first time since I became a Believer. I have spent hour after hour finding homes for unread novels, biographies, memoirs, and collections of essays, poetry, and letters, and suddenly I can see as never before that we're fine for books at the moment, thanks very much. I came across quite a few of the things that have appeared in the Books Bought column at the top of these pages, and marvelled at my own lack of self-knowledge. When exactly was I going to read Michael B. Oren's no doubt excellent book about the Six-Day War? Or Dylan Thomas's letters? The ways in which a man can kid himself are many and various. Anyway, the football season has restarted, which always reduces book time. Arsenal bought only one player over the summer and sold their captain, so we've got a perilously thin squad, and Chelsea have spent squillions again, and.... The truth is, I'm too worried to begin Hilary Spurling's apparently magnificent biography of Matisse (bought about five years ago, new, in hardback, because I couldn't wait). I won't even be able to think about picking it up until Wenger brings in a new central midfield player. And at the time of writing, there's no sign of that. ★

NOVEMBER 2005

BOOKS BOUGHT:
* *A Little History of the World*—E. H. Gombrich
* *What Good Are the Arts?*—John Carey
* *What I Loved*—Siri Hustvedt
* *Death and the Penguin*—Andrey Kurkov

BOOKS READ:
* *The Trick of It*—Michael Frayn
* *Housekeeping*—Marilynne Robinson
* *Over Tumbled Graves*—Jess Walter
* Unnameable comedy thriller—Anonymous

O n my copy of Michael Frayn's *The Trick of It*, there is a quote from Anthony Burgess that describes the novel as "one of the few books I have read in the last year that has provoked laughter." Initially, it's a blurb that works in just the way the publishers intended. Great, you think. Burgess must have read a lot of books; and both the quote itself and your knowledge of the great man suggest that he wouldn't have chuckled at many of them. So if *The Trick of It* wriggled its way through that forbidding exterior to the Burgess sense of humor, it must be absolutely hilarious, right? But then you start to wonder just how trustworthy Burgess would have been on the subject of comedy. What, for example, would have been his favorite bit of *Jackass: The Movie*? (Burgess died in 1993, so sadly we will never know.) What was his most cherished *Three Stooges* sketch? His favorite *Seinfeld* character? His top David Brent moment? And after careful contemplation, your confidence in his comic judgment starts to feel a little misplaced: there is a good chance, you suspect, that Anthony Burgess would have steadfastly refused even to smile at many of the things that have ever made you chortle uncontrollably.

Sometimes it feels as though we are being asked to imagine cultural judgments as a whole bunch of concentric circles. On the outside, we have the wrong ones, made by the people who read *The Da Vinci Code* and listen to Celine Dion; right at the center we have the correct ones, made by the snootier critics, very often people who have vowed never to laugh again until Aristophanes produces a follow-up to *The Frogs*. (I haven't read James Wood's collection of essays *The Irresponsible Self: On Laughter and the Novel,* but I'm counting on Woody to provide a useful counterbalance to that sort of high moral seriousness. So I'm presuming that all the comic greats—P. G. Wodehouse, the Molesworth books, George and Weedon Grossmith, and so on—are present and correct between its covers.) The world is a lot more complicated than this diagram allows, of course, but sometimes it's easy to forget that the Frog people don't know everything. If I had to choose between a Celine Dion fan and Anthony Burgess for comedy recommendations, I would go with the person standing on the table singing *The Power of Love* every time. I'll bet Burgess read *Candide*—I had a bad experience with *Candide* only recently—with tears of mirth trickling down his face.

As you may have guessed by now, *The Trick of It* didn't make me laugh, so I'm feeling insecure. It's brilliant—witty, smart, readable, and engaging; but you know that bit in *Jackass: The Movie* when the guy takes a crap in the bathroom shop? Well, gags of that quality are conspicuously absent. I suspect that it wasn't Michael

Frayn's intention to provide them, either; I raise the comparison only because when you see the word "funny" all over a paperback (Burgess was not alone in having his ribs tickled), it raises expectations to a possibly unrealistic level. *The Trick of It* is about the relationship between a young college professor and his area of expertise, a middle-aged woman novelist he refers to as JL. This relationship becomes complicated, although perhaps in some ways simplified, when he sleeps with her and then marries her: he thus becomes a part of his own research material, a chapter in her still unwritten biography. We have objected to novels about writers and writing in this column before, have we not? We are concerned that the preciousness to which these novels can be prone will alienate the last few readers left out there. But we have no complaints in this case, you and Michael Frayn will be delighted to hear. *The Trick of It* has a healthy resonance rather than a sickly insularity—anyone who has ever been a fan will recognize something in here—and if you've read Frayn's work then you will know how effortlessly clever he is, and thus you can imagine the fun he has with the hall of mirrors he has rigged up here.

I've been reading *Housekeeping* off and on since I finished Marilynne Robinson's second novel, *Gilead,* a while back, but I kept losing it and getting distracted, and in the end I put it down for a while because I was being disrespectful to a novel that people clearly love. I thought I knew what *Housekeeping* would be because I've seen Bill Forsyth's lovely film adaptation a couple of times; I thought it would be warm and quirky, like the movie, except with better prose. Indeed, during the floods in Louisiana I nearly stopped reading the book again, for the hundredth time, because there is a description of a flood right at the beginning of the book, and I was worried that warmth and quirkiness would jar, fight horribly with the scenes we were seeing on the news. So I wasn't prepared for what I actually got, which was this extraordinary, yearning mystical work about the dead and how they haunt the living; if books can work as music, then *Housekeeping* served as a soundtrack to the footage from New Orleans. The dead haunting the living, the core of the book.... That was missing from the movie, as far as I remember. I'm not sure Bill Forsyth knew what to do about all the souls at the bottom of the lake, so he concentrated on his eccentric central characters, and how a small community finds this eccentricity hard to accommodate. It's a fine, slightly conventional theme, but now that I've read the book, I can see that this is rather like making attractive ashtrays out of Kryptonite.

One of the souls at the bottom of the lake belongs to the mother of Ruth, the novel's teenage narrator, and of her sister Lucille; Helen drove into the lake, calmly and deliberately, when her daughters were young. Her father, the girls' grandfather, is down there somewhere too, along with the passengers on a train that came off the bridge that crosses the water. Ruth and Lucille never knew their father, so eventually their aunt Sylvie comes to live with them. She's not much of a mother figure, Sylvie. She sits in the dark surrounded by empty tin cans and old newspapers, and yearns to go back to traveling around on the railroads, but she stays anyway. Have you ever seen that great Stanley Spencer picture, *The Resurrection, Cookham*? It depicts the dead coming alive again, sleepy and bewildered, in the small, pretty, and (otherwise) unremarkable Thameside village where Spencer lived. I'm sure that Robinson must have had the painting in some part of her extraordinary mind when she wrote *Housekeeping*. There is that same strange fusion of the humdrum and the visionary, and though Fingerbone, the bleak little town where the novel is set, clearly isn't as cute as Cookham, it still seems an unlikely location for waking dreams about a reunion of the living and all the people we have ever lost. ("Families should stay together," says Sylvie at the end of the book. "Otherwise things get out of control. My father, you know. I can't even remember what he was like, I mean when he was alive. But ever since, it's Papa here and Papa there, and dreams.")

It's quite clear to me now, having read her two novels, that Marilynne Robinson is one of America's greatest living writers, and certainly there's no one else like her. I think I am using that phrase literally: I have never come across a mind like this one, in literature or anywhere else, for that matter. Sometimes her singular seriousness, and her insistent concentration on the sad beauty of our mortality, make you laugh, in an Anthony Burgess kind of way. Pools and ponds and lakes "taste a bit of blood and hair," observes Ruth, with customary Robinsonian good cheer. "One cannot cup one's hand and drink from the rim of any lake without remembering that mothers have drowned in it, lifting their children toward the air, though they must have known as they did that soon enough the deluge would take all the children, too, even if their arms could have held them up." She may be a great writer, but you wouldn't want her on your camping holiday, would you? (I know, I know, that's a cheap joke, and I'm making the schoolboy error of confusing narrator and author; Marilynne Robinson almost certainly spends her camping holidays singing Beach Boys songs and trying to give everyone wedgies.)

We have, from time to time in these pages, expressed our impatience with a certain kind of literary fiction. (By "these pages," I mean the two I'm given. And by "we," I mean "I." The Spree would never express their impatience with literary fiction. In fact, "the duller the better" is engraved on the gates, in enormous letters, at Spree Castle.) To us, it can sometimes seem overwrought, pedestrian, po-faced, monotonous, out of touch; we would argue that literary fiction must take some of the blame for the novel's sad disappearance from the center of our culture. But sometimes, a book just can't help being literary; it can't do anything about its own complication, because its ideas defy simple expression. It took me forever to read *Housekeeping*, but it's not possible to read this short book quickly, because it comes fitted with its own speed bumps: the neo–Old Testament prose, exactly the right language for Robinson's heartbreaking, prophetic images. And I'm glad I wasn't able to race through it, too, because the time I spent with it means that it lives with me still.

I have always prized the accessible over the obscure, but after reading *Housekeeping* I can see that in some ways the easy, accessible novel is working at a disadvantage (not that *Housekeeping* is inaccessible, but it is deep and dark and rich): it's possible to whiz through it without allowing it even to touch the sides, and a bit of side-touching has to happen if a book is going to be properly transformative. If you are so gripped by a book that you want to read it in the mythical single sitting, what chance has it got of making it all the way through the long march to your soul? It'll get flushed out by something else before it's even halfway there. The trouble is that most literary novels don't do anything but touch the sides. They stick to them like sludge, and in the end you have to get the garden hose out. (I have no idea what that might mean. But I had to escape from the metaphor somehow.)

Neither of the other books I read this month were sludgy, at least. I read and loved Jess Walter's *Citizen Vince* recently, so I wanted to check out one of his earlier books. Unlike *Citizen Vince*, *Over Tumbled Graves* belongs firmly within the crime genre, although it's not formulaic—it actually plays cleverly with the serial-killer formula. I enjoyed it a lot, but on the evidence of the recent book, Walter is a writer who is heading for territory that gives him more freedom than genre fiction allows. Under the *Believer* guidelines, the second novel must remain nameless because I hated it so much. I was recommended it by a friend with normally impeccable taste, and he's not alone—my paperback copy contains blurbs from a couple of clever literary figures who really should know better. Is the phrase "Deliciously politically incorrect" used with the same gay abandon in the U.S.? You come across it all the time here, and usually it means, quite simply, that a book or a movie or a TV program is racist and/or sexist and/or homophobic; there is a certain kind of cultural commentator who mysteriously associates these prejudices with a Golden Age during which we were allowed to do lots of things that we are not allowed to do now. (The truth is that there's no one stopping them from doing anything. What they really object to is being recognized as the antisocial pigs they really are.)

Anyway, this book is "deliciously politically incorrect." The narrator, who fancies himself as a cross between James Bond and Bertie Wooster, thinks it's funny to transpose the *rs* and *ls* in dialogue spoken by Chinese people, and has what he clearly regards as sound advice for women in the process of being raped: "lie quite still, try to enjoy it. The choice is a simple one: a brief and possibly not unpleasant invasion of one's physical privacy—or a painful bashing causing the loss of one's good looks and perhaps one's life." There may well have been men like this in the 1970s, when this book was written, but they were not clever men. It would have been torture to listen to them for two minutes at a bus stop, and you certainly don't want to hang around with them while they narrate a whole book. To compound the reader's misery, this narrator favors a jocular, florid circumlocution intended to invoke the spirit of Wodehouse, who is unwisely mentioned twice in the first fifty pages. I ended up hurling him across the room. At the time of writing, I haven't been able to confront the friend who recommended the book, but there will, I'm afraid, be bloodshed.

I really want to read every book I bought this month. That's true of every month, of course, and usually nothing happens, but this month I really *really* want to read the books I bought. I have just been to a wonderful literary festival in Iceland, where I spent time with Siri Hustvedt and Andrey Kurkov and lots of other interesting, companionable writers; and it's true that there is a slight possibility, judging from my track record, that either of these novels

might fall off the bedside pile at some stage in the future, but surely they can see that the commitment is there? And the two works
of nonfiction, by John Carey and Ernst Gombrich, have the most
perfect titles imaginable: I desperately need to know what the uses
of the arts are, and the great John Carey, who wrote the great *The
Intellectuals and the Masses,* is undoubtedly the man to tell me, and
thus make me feel better about the ways in which I waste my time.
He may even tell me that I'm not wasting my time, as long as he
manages to get solitaire and football under the arts umbrella. The
title of Gombrich's book, meanwhile, cleverly isolates the precise
area in which I am most ignorant. How did he know? ✶

FEBRUARY 2006

BOOKS BOUGHT:

* *Eminent Churchillians*
—Andrew Roberts
* *The Holy Fox: A Biography of Lord Halifax*
—Andrew Roberts
* *The Tender Bar*
—J. R. Moehringer
* *The Brief and Frightening Reign of Phil*
—George Saunders
* *Only in London*
—Hanan Al-Shaykh
* *Traffics and Discoveries*
—Rudyard Kipling
* *The Man Who Was Thursday*
—G. K. Chesterton
* *Ghosting*—Jennie Erdal
* *Untold Stories*
—Alan Bennett
* *Selected Letters of Philip Larkin, 1940–1985*
—Philip Larkin (ed. Anthony Thwaite)
* *Scenes from Life*
—William Cooper

BOOKS READ:

* *Selected Letters of Philip Larkin, 1940–1985*
—Philip Larkin (ed. Anthony Thwaite)
* *On Beauty*—Zadie Smith
* *Five Days in London, May 1940*—John Lukacs
* *All the King's Men*
—Robert Penn Warren
* *Only in London*
—Hanan Al-Shaykh
* *What Good Are the Arts?*
—John Carey
* *The Man Who Was Thursday*
—G. K. Chesterton

I f, as a recent survey in the U.K. suggested, most people buy books because they like to be *seen* reading rather than because they actually enjoy it, then I would suggest that you can't beat a collection of letters by an author—and if that author is a poet, then so much the better. The implication is clear: you know the poet's work inside out (indeed, what you're saying is that if you read his or her entire oeuvre one more time, then the lines would ring round and round in your head like a Kelly Clarkson tune), and you now need something else, something that might help to shed some light on some of the more obscure couplets.

So there I am, reading Larkin's letters every chance I get, and impressing the hell out of anyone who spots me doing so. (Never mind that I never go anywhere, and that therefore the only person likely to spot me doing so is my partner, who at the time I'm most likely to be reading Larkin's letters is very much a sleeping partner.) And what I'm actually reading is stuff like this: "Katherine Mansfield is a cunt." "I think this [poem] is really bloody cunting fucking good." "I have just made up a rhyme: After a particularly good game of rugger / A man called me a bugger / Merely because in a loose scrum / I had my cock up his bum." "Your letter found me last night when I came in off the piss: in point of fact I had spewed out of a train window and farted in the presence of ladies and generally misbehaved myself." And so on. In other words, you get to have your cake and eat it: you look like *un homme ou femme sérieux/sérieuse,* but you feel like a twelve-year-old who's somehow being allowed to read *Playboy* in an English lesson. And what you come to realize is that the lifestyle of a naughty twelve-year-old is enervating to the max, if you're a grown-up; indeed, there are quite a few thirteen-year-olds who would find great chunks of Larkin's correspondence embarrassingly puerile.

The irony is that I was drawn to Larkin's letters through that beautiful poem "Church Going," which makes a case for the value of churches long after organized religion has lost its appeal and its point: "And that much never can be obsolete / Since someone will forever be surprising / A hunger in himself to be more serious." This last line was quoted in an article I was reading in the *Economist,* of all places, and it struck a post-*Gilead* chord with me, so I reread a few of the poems and then decided that I'd like access to the prose version of the mind that created them. And yes, you can see where Larkin's hunger to become more serious came from; if I had a mouth like that, I'd have wanted to pay frequent visits to God's house, too. Larkin writes brilliantly and enthusiastically about his jazz records, and every now and again there's a peach of a letter about writing:

> Poetry (at any rate in my case) is like trying to remember a tune you've forgotten. All corrections are attempts to get nearer to the forgotten tune. A poem is written because the poet gets a sudden vision—lasting one second or less—and he attempts to express the whole of which the vision is a part.

And that's the sort of thing you want, surely, when you wade through a writer's letters. What you end up with, however, is a lot of stuff about farting and wanking. Every now and again you are reminded forcibly that the ability to write fiction or poetry is not necessarily indicative of a particularly refined intelligence, no matter what we'd like to believe; it's a freakish talent, like the ability to bend a ball into the top corner of the goal from a thirty-yard free kick, but no one's interested in reading Thierry Henry's collected letters—no literary critic, anyway. And Thierry would never call Katherine Mansfield a cunt, not least because he's a big fan of the early stories. Anyway, I have given up on Larkin for the moment. The rest of you: stick to the poems.

As nobody noticed, probably, I was barred from the *Believer* again last month, this time for quoting from one of Philip Larkin's letters, more or less accurately—what's a second-person pronoun between friends?—at an editorial meeting. The Polysyllabic Spree, the seventy-eight repellently evangelical young men and women who run the magazine, "couldn't hear the quotation marks," apparently, and anyway, as they pointed out (somewhat unnecessarily, I felt), I'm no Larkin. So I have a lot of ground to cover here—I have had several Major Reading Experiences over the last couple of months, and I've got to cram them all into a couple of measly pages, all because of those teenage white robed prudes. Oh, it's not your problem. I'll just get on with it. I know I won't need to tell you anything about Zadie Smith's warm, moving, smart, and thoroughly enjoyable *On Beauty;* Hanan Al-Shaykh was one of the authors I met on a recent trip to Reykjavik, and her lovely novel *Only in London* was a perfect reflection of the woman: surprising, fun, thoughtful.

A disgruntled Barnesandnoble.com punter slams Robert Penn Warren's *All the King's Men:* "Oh well," says our critic in his one-star review. "At least it was better than the *Odyssey.*" This means, presumably, that the *Odyssey* is a no-star book; you have to admire someone prepared to flout conventional literary wisdom so publicly. I personally don't agree, and for me the *Odyssey* still has the edge, but Warren's novel seems to have held up pretty well. It's overwritten, here and there—Warren can't see a sunny day without comparing it to a freckly girl wearing a polka-dot dress and new shoes, sitting on a fence clutching a strawberry lollipop and whistling—and at one point, apropos almost nothing, there's a thirty-page story set during the Civil War which seems to belong to another book altogether. You could be forgiven for thinking that *All the King's Men* could have done with a little more editing, rather than a little less; but the edition I read is a new "restored" edition of the novel, containing a whole bunch of stuff—a hundred pages, apparently—that were omitted from the version originally published. A hundred pages! Oh, dear God. Those of us still prepared to pick up sixty-year-old Pulitzer Prize–winners should be rewarded, not horribly and unfairly punished.

You may well already have read *All the King's Men;* you will, therefore, be familiar with Willie Stark, Penn's central character, a demagogic Southern politician whose rise and demise deliberately recalls that of Huey Long. Me, I've just read a book about someone called Willie Talos—the name Warren originally wanted until he was talked out of it by his editor. I think the editor was right; as Joyce Carol Oates said in her *NYRB* piece about the restored edition, "'Talos' is a showy, pretentious, rather silly name in the 'Stephen Dedalus' tradition, while 'Willie Stark' is effective without being an outright nudge in the ribs." But even that, I don't think, is the point; the point is that Willie Stark is now the character's name, whatever the author intended all those years ago, and whichever name is better is a moot point. I feel as though I've just read a book about David Copperbottom or Holden Calderwood or Jay Gatsbergen. You can't mess around with that stuff, surely? These people exist independently of the books, now—I have, I now realize, seen countless references to Willie Stark in reviews and magazine articles, but as the book isn't widely known or read here in the U.K., I had no idea that was who I was reading about until after I'd finished.

Talos was, apparently, the guardian of Crete, who threw boulders at people attempting to land on the island; he was also a mechanical man attendant on the Knight of Justice in Spenser's "Faerie Queene." These are both very good reasons why Talos is a very bad name for a Southern American politician, I would have thought, and I can imagine that a good editor would have made the same arguments. Noel Polk, who put this new edition together, is of the opinion that Warren was badly served by the editing process; in a reply to Joyce Carol Oates's piece, he claims that "many of us are interested in more than a good read," and that he knows, and Oates doesn't, "how often well-intentioned commercial editors have altered novels for the worse." If I were Robert Penn Warren's editor, I'd point to a Pulitzer Prize and sixty years in print as all the vindication I needed; we will never know whether Polk's version would ever have endured anywhere near as well. There is even the possibility, of course, that if Warren had had his way in 1947, there would have been no interest in any kind of edition in the twenty-first century. I can see that scholars might

want to compare and contrast, but I notice on Amazon that the
long 'un I read now has a movie tie-in cover. Caveat emptor.

I reread John Lukacs's little book on what turned out to be the
biggest decision of the twentieth century—namely, Churchill's
decision not to seek terms with Hitler in May 1940—because
I found it on my bookshelf and realized that the only thing I could
remember was Churchill deciding not to seek terms with Hitler
in 1940. And I kind of knew that bit before I read it. So this time,
I'm going to make a few notes that help make it all stick—it's
great, having this column, because I keep the magazines, but I'd
probably lose a notebook. Excuse me a moment. Norway defeat
brings down Chamberlain; C becomes PM 5/10/1940. Early
unpopularity of C in his own party—"blood, sweat, toil, and tears"
speech didn't go down well—"gangsters" + "rogue elephant."
Churchill v HALIFAX. Churchill and Lloyd George—wanted
him in the Cabinet because LG admired Hitler, who might
appoint him if and when... Dunkirk: feared max 50,000
evacuated—in the end over 338,000.

Thanks. That'll really help.

Lukacs's book is completely gripping, clear, and informative,
and corroborates a theory I've been developing recently: the less
there is to say about something, the more opaque the writing
tends to be. In other words, you hardly ever come across an
unreadable book on World War II, but pick up a book on, I don't
know, the films of Russ Meyer, and you'll be rereading the same
impossible sentence about poststructuralist auteurism three hundred times. People have to overcompensate, you see. And *Five Days
in London* also helped give a context for Philip Larkin's early letters, too. Here's Larkin, in 1942: "If there is any new life in the
world today, it is in Germany." "Germany will win this war like a
dose of salts" (1940). "And I agree we don't deserve to win"
(1942). Lukacs points out that there was a grudging admiration for
Hitler's Germany in Britain: we were clapped-out, the old order,

whereas Germany was thrusting, energetic, modern. And he also notes that it was the intellectuals—and I suppose Larkin must be categorized thus, despite the farting—who were most prone to defeatism. Ha! That's the Spree, right there. They're very brave when it comes to suspending innocent columnists. But you wait until someone (and my money is on the French) lands on the West Coast. You won't see them for dust.

And the coveted "Stuff I've Been Reading: Stuff That Stayed Read" award for the nonfiction book of 2005 goes to... John Carey, for *What Good Are the Arts?* It's rare, I think, for a writer, maybe for anyone, to feel that he's just read a book that absolutely expresses who he or she is, and what he or she believes, while at the same time recognizing that he or she could not have written any of it. But Carey's book—which in its first two chapters answers the questions "What is a work of art?" and "Is high art superior?"—is my new bible, replacing my previous bible, Carey's *The Intellectuals and the Masses.* I couldn't have written it because I—and I'm not alone, by any means—do not have Carey's breadth of reading, nor his calm, wry logic, which enables him to demolish the arguments of just about everyone who has ever talked tosh about objective aesthetic principles. And this group, it turns out, includes anyone who has ever talked about objective aesthetic principles, from Kant onwards. *What Good Are the Arts?* is a very wise book, and a very funny book, but beyond even these virtues, it's a very humane, inclusive, and empathetic book: as we all know, it's impossible to talk about "high" art without insulting the poor, or the young, or those without a university degree, or those who have no taste for, or interest in, Western culture. Carey's approach to the whole sorry mess is the only one that makes any sense. Indeed, while reading it, you become increasingly amazed at the muddle that apparently intelligent people have got themselves into when they attempt to define the importance of—and the superiority of—"high" culture.

Just after I'd finished it, and I was looking at the world through

Carey's eyes, the winner of the 2005 Booker Prize claimed that at least his was a "proper" book—as if *Green Eggs and Ham* or *Bridget Jones's Diary* weren't proper books. And then, a few days later, the *Guardian's* art correspondent launched an astonishing attack on the popular British artist Jack Vettriano: "Vettriano is not even an artist." (No, he's just someone who paints pictures and sells them. What do you call those people again?) "He just happens to be popular, with 'ordinary people'.... I'm not arguing with you, I'm telling you.... Some things about art are true, and some are false— all of which was easier to explain before we decided popularity was the litmus test of aesthetic achievement...."

Oh, man. That's got it all. This is not the time or the place to unravel the snobbery and the unexamined assumptions contained in those few lines; it's easier just to say that nothing about art is true, and nothing is false. And if that's scary, then I'm sorry, but you have to get over it and move on.

I read G. K. Chesterton's *The Man Who Was Thursday* because (*a*) I'd never read a word by Chesterton and (*b*) because I'd decided that from now on I'd only read stuff that John Carey recommends (in his useful little book *Pure Pleasure*). And it was pretty good, although I think that younger readers might get a little frustrated with the plotting. I don't want to give too much away. But say you were an *x,* and you believed that a group of seven people were all not *x*s but *y*s. And then you discovered that the first of these seven was actually an *x,* too. And then you found out the same thing about the second, and then the third. Wouldn't you start to get the idea? Yes, well. Anyway, I can't say anything else about it now other than that it's a novel that fundamentally believes in the decency and the wisdom of us all, and you don't find too many of those. John Carey has now made me buy a book by Kipling, and I didn't think anyone would ever manage that. ✷

MARCH 2006

BOOKS BOUGHT:
* *Eustace and Hilda*
  —L. P. Hartley
* *Hang-Ups*
  —Simon Schama
* *Scenes from Metropolitan
  Life*—William Cooper

BOOKS READ:
* *Scenes from Provincial
  Life*—William Cooper
* *Scenes from Metropolitan
  Life*—William Cooper
* *Death and the Penguin*
  —Andrey Kurkov
* *Ghosting*—Jennie Erdal

So this last month was, as I believe you people say, a bust. I had high hopes for it, too; It was Christmas time in England, and I was intending to do a little holiday comfort reading—*David Copperfield* and a couple of John Buchan novels, say, while sipping an eggnog and....

Oh, what's the point? No one, I suppose, will remember that I began my March '05 column in this way. And if no one remembers me beginning my March '05 in this way, then there is even less chance of them remembering that I began my March '04 column in this way too. The tragedy is that I have come to think of those opening words as a tradition, and I was beginning to hope that you have come to value them as such. I even had a little fantasy that one of your popular entertainers—Stephen Sondheim, say, or Puff Diddle—might have set them to music, and at the beginning of March you all hold hands and sing a song called "It Was Christmas Time in England," to mark the imminent arrival of spring. I am beginning to suspect, however, that this column is making only medium-sized inroads into the American consciousness. (I have had very little feedback from readers in Alabama, for example, and not much more from our Hawaiian subscribers.) I shall keep the tradition going, but more in hope than expectation. It's the New Year here in England, and I'm sorry to say that, because of the apparent indifference of both Puff Diddle and Alabama (the whole state, rather than the band), I am entering 2006 on a somewhat self-doubting and ruminative note.

This last reading month really was a wash-out, though, for all the usual holiday reasons, so it was as well that, with incredible and atypical foresight, I held a couple of books back from the previous month, just to pad the column out a bit. I met Andrey Kurkov at the Reykjavik Literary Festival, and loved the reading he gave from *Death and the Penguin*. (He also sat at the piano and sang a few jolly Ukrainian songs afterwards, thus wilfully and sacriligiously puncturing the solemnity of the occasion. You can't mess around with readings by singing after them. The paying public might begin to expect fun at literary events, and then where would writers be? Up shit creek without a paddle, that's where.) I afterwards discovered that *Death and the Penguin* is one of those books that people love unreservedly. The eyes of the assistant in the bookshop lit up when I bought it, and all sorts of people have shown a frankly sickening devotion to the novel whenever I've mentioned it since.

I think I'd sort of presumed that the eponymous penguin was metaphorical, like both the squid and the whale in *The Squid and the Whale;* my antipathy to the animal kingdom is such that even animal metaphors tend to have a deterrent effect. (What kind of person thinks in animal metaphors? In this day and age?) Imagine my horror, then, when I learned during Kurkov's reading in Reykjavik that the penguin in *Death and the Penguin* is not like the squid or the whale, but, like, an actual penguin. The penguin really is a character, who—pull yourself together, man, *which*—has moods and feelings, and has an integral part in the story, and so on. And, as if the author actually wanted me to hate his novel, it's a cute penguin, too. "It will be a hard-hearted reader who is not touched by Viktor's relationship with his unusual pet," says one of the quotes on the back. (Why not just find a blurb saying "DON'T BUY THIS BOOK"?) And, of course, *Death and the Penguin* turns out to be fresh, funny, clever, incredibly soulful and compelling, and the penguin turns out to be a triumphant creation. I might only read books about animals from now on.

Misha is effectively Viktor's flatmate; he adopted it (I'm not giving in on the pronoun thing) when the failing local zoo was dishing out animals to whoever could afford to feed them, and as Viktor's girlfriend had recently moved out, he was feeling lonely. (Oh, stop it. It's not that sort of book.) Misha, however, turns out to be as depressed as Viktor, and it just sort of wanders about, and occasionally disappears off to its bedroom, like a homesick teenager on a foreign exchange program. Viktor, meanwhile, has recently started work as an obituarist: he's told to write and stockpile the obituaries of leading local figures, but the obits turn out to be needed earlier than anticipated, and Viktor eventually realizes that his is somehow bringing about the untimely demise of his subjects.

It's a neat plot, but *Death and the Penguin* isn't a plotty book: Kurkov gives himself plenty of room to breathe (it's actually more of a long, rueful sigh) and that's pretty cool in and of itself. This is a literary novel—Kurkov loves his *weltschmerz* as much as the next guy—but he doesn't see why weltschmerz shouldn't come bundled up with a narrative that kicks a little bit of ass—the edge of the left cheek, say. Sometimes it seems as though everything in the arts (and I include sports in the arts) is about time and space—giving yourself room to move, finding the time to play.... My copy of *Death and the Penguin* is two hundred and twenty-eight pages long, and yet it never seems overstuffed, or underpowered, and it manages to be about an awful lot, and it never ever forgets or overlooks gesture or detail. And I already said it was funny, didn't I? What more do you want? At that length, you couldn't even reasonably want less.

Jennie Erdal's *Ghosting* is a book about writing, so, you know, if you don't want to read it because you're a plumber or a chiropodist, then I quite understand. If I were you, I would resent the repeated implication, by publishers and books pages, that my profession is more interesting than yours. Unlike most books about writing, though, this one contains a narrative that is both genuinely gripping and eccentric. Jennie Erdal was employed by a flamboyant London publisher, the sort of man who is often described as "larger than life." (In other words, run for the hills! And don't look back!) She began as a translator, and then worked on a huge book of interviews this guy conducted with women; finally, she wrote two novels for him. They were his novels—his name, and his name alone, was on the title page—but according to Erdal, the author took only a passing interest in their conception and execution.

His first novel, he decides, will be both thrilling and very romantic: "It has to be a love story. People associate me with love..." When his amanuensis asks whether he has any notion of the characters who might populate this thrilling love story, he is precise and unequivocal: they must be "a man and a woman. Do you think I could write about poofters?"

So away Jennie Erdal goes, and writes a novel, and the flamboyant publisher publishes it, and it gets respectful reviews—partly because the flamboyant publisher is a respected figure, and partly, one suspects, because Erdal can clearly write. And, rather than breathe a huge sigh of relief, he decides to "write" another, although this one turns out to have a higher, tighter concept than the first: he wants it to be about two women, cousins born on the same day, who are so close that when one achieves orgasm, so does the other. Pretty good, you have to admit, and as Erdal seems, inexplicably, to have ignored the idea, it's still going begging.

Ghosting is a strange and rather wonderful book, and it makes you think about all sorts of things connected with writing and the notion of authorship. The truth is, however, that it's old news. Almost nobody writes their own books these days; indeed, to do so is seen as a mark of failure in literary circles. Of course, the young have no choice, and there are, apparently, a few renegades who insist on churning out word after word: the word on the literary street is that Michael Chabon wrote every word of *The Amazing Adventures of Kavalier and Clay*, for example, presumably out of some misguided and outdated notion of honesty. But the rest of us don't really bother. I have always used an old lady called Violet, who lives in a cottage in Cornwall, in the far west of England, and who is an absolute treasure. She's getting better, too.

For some reason, I found myself up a ladder in Strand Books in New York a couple of months ago, looking to see whether they had any copies of old William Cooper novels. I know that Philip Larkin mentions him in his letters, but there may have been another nudge from somewhere, too. Whatever the motivation, I was led as if by magic to a beautiful 1961 Scribners hardback which cost me six dollars, and which contained Cooper's first and third novels, *Scenes From Provincial Life* and *Scenes from Married Life*, published in the U.S. as *Scenes from Life*.

I'd read them both before, twenty or more years ago, and I remembered them as being particularly important to me, although I wouldn't have been able to articulate why. Now I can see it: Joe Lunn, the hero of these books (and Cooper's thinly disguised alter-ego) is, in the first book at least, a schoolteacher who has ambitions to make his living from writing, and that's exactly the situation I found myself in when my sister gave me the books as a Christmas present in what must have been '82 or '83, seeing as those were the only years I was in full-time gainful employment in a school. I don't think I managed to see the connection at the time. Really. I thought I'd been enjoying them for other reasons. (They are incredibly enjoyable books.) I thought I should own up to that, just to help you gauge the soundness of all the other literary judgements I make on these pages.

The reason that *Scenes from Metropolitan Life,* the second novel in the sequence, isn't included in the edition I bought is that it wasn't published until 1982, even though it was written in the 1950s; Cooper's work was so autobiographical that he was threatened with legal action by the real-life version of the young woman who is Joe's girlfriend in the first book and his mistress in the second. (Is that right? The thing is, she gets married in between the two, although he doesn't. Can you have a mistress if you're not married? Can you be a mistress if your lover isn't married? Is there a useful handbook you can look these things up in?) Publication of *Scenes From Metropolitan Life* was only possible after her death, and in the meantime Cooper's career had lost all the momentum it built up after the success of the first novel. All his books are out of print now.

Scenes From Provincial Life is a lovely novel, sweet-natured, and surprisingly frank about sexual relationships, considering the book is set in 1939: Joe has a weekend cottage which he shares with a friend, and where a lot of the book is set. Joe sleeps with Myrtle, the litiginous girlfriend, there; Joe's friend Tom uses it for trysts with his seventeen-year-old boyfriend Steve. See what I mean? Who knew anyone had sex in 1939, in a provincial town? Well, we all did, I suppose, but in Larkin's words, "sexual intercourse began in 1963"—or at least, twentieth-century mainstream British artistic representations of it did—so it's weird to read what is effectively a Kingsley Amis-style comedy of sexual manners which also talks about Chamberlain at Munich.

If *Scenes From Metropolitan Life* is a little less successful, it's partly because all the characters are a little older, and a little sadder, and they take their jobs more seriously, and those jobs are a little more dull: Joe is a civil servant in the second book. He's still trying to make up his mind whether to marry Myrtle, but Myrtle's married already, to someone stationed in Palestine, and Cooper's insouciance doesn't really seem to take the sadness of any of that onboard. (My pristine second-hand copy came from my Amazon marketplace seller with Kingsley Amis's 1982 *Sunday Times* review tucked neatly into the dust-jacket, by the way. Kingsley loved the first one, but gave the second a reluctant thumbs-down.) I've just started the third, and Joe's nearly forty, still single, and still looking, and you're beginning to suspect that there might actually be something wrong with him that he's not owning up to. It's hard, trying to be funny about getting older. *Scenes From Provincial Life* can afford to be cute and fresh because the characters have so little at stake; but then we grow older, more tired, more cynical, more worried; and then we die. And where's the joke in that? Oh. Ha. I've just seen it. It's pretty good.

Happy March, dear *Believer* readers. I hope you have a fantastic ten months. ★

A selection from

GHOSTING

by JENNIE ERDAL

It is 1994 and we are off to France once again. This time we are going there to write a novel. The publication of several non-fiction books has brought Tiger a sense of fulfilment, but there has been no lasting contentment. As the ancients knew and understood, pleasure is transient; it comes, it is savored, and it goes. Descartes thought that the secret of happiness was to be satisfied with what you know you can have, and not to hanker after something you can't have. But Tiger differs from both the ancients and Descartes in his belief that almost anything is attainable provided you pay for it, and that by setting the sights high the chances of pleasure being permanent are correspondingly high.

And so, from one moment to the next, anything can happen. A moment ago a sixth volume of interviews was published, attended by a good deal of media interest, favourable reviews, and another round of newspaper profiles. In the *Daily Telegraph* Allan Massie described Tiger as "masterly and sympathetic, the most self-effacing of interviewers and yet able to speak as an equal." Robert Kee called him "a magician interviewer of the highest order." William Trevor wrote: "Making real people real at second hand isn't as easy as it seems… it's the subtlety of interrogation that ensures these portraits emerge." Tiger purred with pleasure. Everything was well in the world. The next moment we are writing a novel and the landscape has changed. *Sic transit Gloria mundi*.

Tiger is convinced that the way ahead "for us" lies in a different sort of publication. Interviews, newspaper articles, book reviews are all very well, but *the real test* is the novel. He lowers his voice at this point, enunciating each word slowly, a sure sign of scarcely being able to contain his excitement, elongating the word *real* to a disturbing length. He is captivated by the idea. This is not a whim. I know the difference between a whim and a serious proposition. This is a serious proposition. He will not be dissuaded. The tiger is not for turning. I feel the familiar panic pitching its tent somewhere in my lower abdomen.

"We need to evolve," he says.

I do not demur.

How to write a novel? How to write someone else's novel? These two questions seem absolutely central. I wonder how I have arrived at this point without actually meaning to.

"What sort of novel are we thinking about?" I ask.

We are in the British Airways Executive Lounge at London Gatwick airport en route to France. The writing will be done in France. According to Tiger, France is the best place in the world to create a work of literature. Evidently we will have everything we need: the best food, the finest wine, a high-tech music system, a studio to work in, the fresh Dordogne air.

"We are thinking about a beautiful novel, very beautiful," he says, and he looks somewhere into the middle distance, smiling rapturously, already transported by the sheer imagined beauty of it. "And it will have a beautiful cover. We will make sure of that." He taps out the last six words on the table.

"But what genre are we talking about? Are we thinking of a romantic novel? A thriller?" (These conversations are always conducted in the first person plural. The idiosyncratic use of pronouns is part of the charade and has become second nature.)

"It will be thrilling, oh yes. And also romantic. *Very* romantic. Oh, yes."

"So, a love story then?"

"But of course! It *has* to be a love story. People associate me with love. I am *famous* for love. Isn't it?"

In certain circumstances, the plural pronoun would switch abruptly to the singular, from *we* to *I*, from *us* to *me*. There is always a compelling reason for the shift. In this instance, the snag is that people do not associate *me* with love. Unlike Tiger, I am not famous for love.

There is a long pause. The matter might have ended there, but for my need to establish the broad nature of the project. I have to ask some more. Tiger is almost certainly concentrating on the finished product, beautifully bound and wrapped in a seductive dust-jacket. My only concern is how the finished product will be arrived at.

"What sort of love story do we have in mind?' I ask, as if we are discussing wallpaper or home furnishings and he has to pick one from a limited range. "Is the love requited or unrequited?"

"Definitely requited. Oh yes, very requited."

"And who are the characters?"

Even by our standards this is becoming an odd exchange.

"Sweetie," he says, the tone long-suffering, humouring an imbecile. He takes hold of my hand in a kindness-to-dumb-animals sort of way. "It *has* to be the love between a man and a woman. Do you think I could write about *poofters*? No, it has to be a man and a woman—a beautiful woman and very sexy. There will be lots of sex, but very distinguished. We will do the sex beautifully. Isn't it?"

"Long? Short?" I'm feeling desperate now.

He strokes his chin, weighing up the possibilities.

"Not too long, not too short."

"And do we have a story line? Do we have any idea of what it is *about*?"

"Of course, beloved! I have thought of *everything*." He squeals the last word in a spasm of exuberance. "Let me tell you the idea. It is very simple. There is a man... he is like me somewhat... he is married... he falls in love with a woman... there is a *huge* passion... and then... well, we will see what happens after that, isn't it?"

There is another pause while I weight things up. Then:

"Does he tell his wife? About the huge passion, I mean."

"Darling, are you *mad*?" Tiger points a finger to his template and screws it from side to side. "Why would he tell her? Why would he hurt her?" ✷

APRIL 2006

"Character *is fate."* Discuss with reference to Eustace Cher-rington *in* The Shrimp and the Anemone *and Nikki Sixx in* The Dirt.

(It occurred to me that with the exam season coming up, younger readers might actually prefer this format for the column. I don't know how many of you are studying L. P. Hartley's *The Shrimp and the Anemone* in conjunction with *The Dirt*—probably not many. But even if it's only a couple of hundred, I'll feel as though I've provided some kind of public service. Please feel free to lift as much of the following as you need.)

In many ways, Eustace Cherrington—the younger half of the

brother-sister combo in Hartley's *Eustace and Hilda* trilogy—and Nikki Sixx, the Crue's bass player, are very different people. Eustace is a young boy, and Nikki Sixx is a grown man; Eustace is English, middle-class, and fictional, and Nikki Sixx is working-class, American, and (according to the internet at least) a real person. *The Shrimp and the Anemone* is a very beautiful novel, full of delicate people and filigree observation, whereas *The Dirt* is possibly the ugliest book ever written. And yet Eustace and Nikki Sixx both, each in their own ways, somehow manage to disprove Heraclitus's maxim—or at any rate, they demand its modification. Both Hartley's novel and the Crüe bio remind us it's not *character* but *constitution* that determine our destinies. Eustace is, let's face it, a weed and a wuss. He's got a weak heart, so he can't go out much, and when he eventually steels himself to take part in a paper chase with the delectable but destructive Nancy, he collapses with exhaustion and takes to his sickbed for months. Nikki Sixx, however, is made of sterner stuff. When he ODs on heroin in L.A. and nearly dies—a journalist phones one of his bandmates for an obituary—what does he do? He gets home, pulls a lump of heroin out of the medicine cabinet, and ODs again. Thus we can see that Nikki Sixx and Eustace Cherrington live the lives that their bodies allow them to live. Nothing really matters, apart from this. Why do some of us read a lot of books and watch a lot of TV instead of play in Mötley Crüe? Because we haven't got the stomachs for it. It's as simple as that.

It was a mistake, reading *The Dirt* straight after *The Shrimp and the Anemone*. (Is it just a coincidence, by the way, that whole shrimp/anemone/squid/whale combo? Because even though Hartley's sea creatures are little ones, unlike writer-director Noah Baumbach's monsters, they serve pretty much the same metaphorical function: the novel opens with a gruesome and symbolic battle to the death. Anyway, where's the meat? Can anyone think of a way to get a little artistic surf'n'turf action going?) *The Dirt* shat and puked and pissed all over the memory of poor Eustace's defenseless introspection—indeed, so grotesque are the characters and narrative events described in the Mötley Crüe book that it's very difficult to see any ideal circumstance in which to read it. I certainly recommend not reading anything for a month before, because the strong flavors of Nikki, Tommy Lee, and the other two will overwhelm pretty much any other literary delicacy you may have consumed; and you probably won't want to read any fiction for a month afterward because it will be hard to see the point. There are moments in *The Dirt* that render any attempts to explain the intricate workings of the human heart redundant, because there are no intricate workings of the human heart, clearly. There are only naked groupies, and endless combinations of class A drugs, and booze, and covers of "Smokin' in the Boys' Room." And what have you got to say about all that, Anita Brookner? No. I thought not. There is one moment in *The Dirt* so disturbingly repellent that it haunts me still, but I'm unsure whether to quote it or not, for obvious reasons. What I think I'll do is reproduce the offending line in tiny writing, and if you want to read it, you'll have to go and fetch a magnifying glass—that way, you have participated in your own corruption. I advise you not to bother. This, then, from the early days:

We'd scrounge up enough money to buy an egg burrito from Noggles. Then we'd buy the rest off and stick our dicks into the warm meat to cover up the smell of puss, so that our girlfriends didn't know we were fucking anything stupid or drunk enough to get into Tommy's van.

I'm afraid I have various questions about this. In America, are showers not cheaper than egg burritos? Does Noggles itself (we don't even have the establishment here in England, let alone the Noggles-associated behavior) not have a washroom? And didn't the girlfriends ever wonder... actually, forget it. We've gone far enough. It could be, of course, that this episode is a fabrication, but without wishing to add to the contemporary furor about the falsification of real lives, I'd argue that this is of a whole new order: anyone depraved enough to imagine this is certainly depraved enough to do it.

So why read it at all? Well, I read it because my friend Erin gave it to me for Christmas, and she had taken quite a lot of trouble to track down a nice hardback copy. Why Erin thought this was an appropriate gift with which to commemorate the birth of our Lord I'm not sure; why she thought that it was an appropriate gift for me is even less clear and somewhat more troubling. Certain passages, it is true, were uncannily reminiscent of certain nights on my last book tour, especially the Midwest readings. I had hoped that what went on there was a secret between me and the women whose names began with the letters A through E (so many broken-hearted Felicitys!) at the signings in question, but clearly not.

And weirdly, *The Dirt* isn't a bad book. For a start, it's definitive, if you're looking for the definitive book on vile, abusive, misogynistic behavior: if there are any worse stories than this in rock and roll, they aren't worth telling, because the human mind would not be capable of comprehending them without the aid of expert gynecological and pharmaceutical assistance. It's very nicely put together, too. *The Dirt* is an oral biography in the tradition of *Please Kill Me,* and Neil Strauss, the Studs Terkel of hair metal, has a good ear for the band's self-delusions, idiocies, and fuckups. Strauss, one suspects, has class. (Wilkie Collins provides the book's epigraph, for example, and I'm guessing that this wasn't Tommy Lee's idea.) "I decided to have the name of the album, *Till Death Do Us Part,* carved into my arm," recalls the hapless John Corabi, who replaced singer Vince Neil for one unsuccessful album. "Soon afterward they changed the name of the album to just *Mötley Crüe.*" Unexpectedly, *The Dirt* contains real pain, too. None of these characters have childhoods that one might envy, and their adult lives seem every bit as bleak and as joyless—especially if you are cursed with a constitution that prevents anything more than an occasional night in the Bank of Friendship.

The real victim here, however, is *The Shrimp and the Anemone,* which never stood a chance. It was fantastic, too. I picked it up after my friend Wesley Stace, whose first novel *Misfortune* has been picking up a distressing amount of attention, recommended it. (Not personally, of course—he's beyond that now. He gave it a mention in a *Guardian* questionnaire.) I'm going to read the whole *Eustace and Hilda* trilogy, and I'll write about it more when I've finished. Suffice to say that after last month's entirely felicitous William Cooper experience, I'm happy with my run of lost mid-century minor classics. And just as, a while back, I vowed only to read things recommended by Professor John Carey, I am now determined only to read things blurbed by John Betjeman. He is quoted on the back of *Eustace and Hilda,* just as he is on *Scenes from Provincial Life,* and on Nigel Balchin's *Darkness Falls from the Air,* purchased this month after a tip-off. He was missing from the jacket of the Crüe book, which should have served as a warning. He clearly didn't like it much.

I was not able to heed my own advice and take time out after rubbing my nose in *The Dirt:* this column, as Nikki Sixx would say, is insatiable, a nymphomaniac, and I had to press on. I couldn't return to Hartley, for obvious reasons, so I went with Michael Connolly's clever serial killer—I needed the moral disgust that thriller writers cannot avoid when dealing with dismembered children, etc. There was one twist too many for me at the end, but other than that, *The Poet* did a difficult post-Crüe job well. I did end up thinking about how evolving technology makes things tough for contemporary crime-writers, though. *The Poet* was first published in 1996 and contains an unfortunate explanation of the concept of digital photography that even my mum would now find redundant; the novel ends with an enigma that DNA testing would render bathetically unenigmatic within seconds. Filmmakers hate setting movies in the recent past, that awkward time when things are neither "period" nor contemporary. The recent past just looks wrong. Characters have cell phones the size of bricks and listen to music on Discmen. The same principle applies here: at these moments, *The Poet* feels anachronistic. Surely people who know their way around a laptop can do a spot of DNA testing? But no. I now see why my thriller-writing brother-in-law has run off to ancient Rome and barricaded himself in. He's not daft.

Still trying to dispel the memory of the egg burrito, I picked up Andrew Smith's *Moondust,* a book about what happened to the astronauts who walked on the moon after they fell to earth, on the grounds that you wouldn't be able to see Nikki Sixx from space. (And even if you could, you wouldn't be able to see what he was doing.) I put it down again in order to read a proof copy of a terrific first novel, Joshua Ferris's *Then We Came to the End.* Young Ferris and I share a publisher, and *Then We Came to the End* came with a ringing endorsement from a colleague. She wasn't after a blurb—she just talked with infectious and intriguing enthusiasm about the book, and this enthusiasm is entirely understandable. This book is going to attract a lot of admiration when it comes out later this year. I'm glad I read it before everybody else, because I would otherwise have been deterred by the hype (and here "hype" is an envious and dismissive substitute for "praise," which is how the word is usually used).

The author will, I suspect, become sick of descriptions of his novel, all of which will use the word "meets," or possibly the phrase "rewritten by." As *Then We Came to the End* has not been published yet, however, he is unlikely to be sick of them yet, so I can splurge. It's *The Office* meets Kafka. It's *Seinfeld* rewritten by Donald Barthelme. It's *Office Space* reimagined by Nicholson… Oh, that'll do. The book is written in the first-person plural (as in "we," for those who never got the hang of declining nouns), and I was reminded of Barthelme because of his two brilliant stories "Our Work and Why We Do It" and "Some of Us Had Been Threatening Our Friend Colby," neither of which is narrated in the first-person plural, but which, as you may have noticed, refer to "us" or "we" in the titles. So you could be forgiven for thinking that the resemblance is somewhat superficial. Barthelme, however, did have the very great gift of being able to make the mundane seem mysterious, and Ferris can do that when he wants to: his novel is set in an advertising office, and the rhythms and substance of a working day are slowly revealed to have the rhythms and substance of life itself. The novel, almost incidentally, feels utterly authentic in its depiction of office life—a rare achievement in fiction, seeing as most writers have never done a proper day's work in their lives—but the authenticity is not the point of it, because underneath the politicking and the sackings and the petty jealousies you can hear something else: the sound of our lives (that collective pronoun again) ticking away. And before I put you off, I should add that the novel is awfully funny, in both senses of the phrase. It's about cancer, totem poles, Emerson, and grief, among many other things, and you should preorder it now. It's our sort of book.

Oh, but what do any of these things matter? Is it really possible that Mötley Crüe have destroyed all the literature in the world, everything that came before them, and everything written since? I rather fear it is. Please don't go looking for that magnifying glass. Save yourself while there's still time. ★

A selection from

THEN WE CAME TO THE END

by JOSHUA FERRIS

★ ★ ★

YOU DON'T KNOW WHAT'S IN MY HEART

We were fractious and overpaid. Our mornings lacked promise. At least those of us who smoked had something to look forward to at ten fifteen. Most of us liked most everyone, a few of us hated specific individuals, one or two people loved everyone and everything. Those who loved everyone were unanimously reviled. We loved free bagels in the morning. They happened all too infrequently. Our benefits were astonishing in comprehensiveness and quality of care. Sometimes we questioned whether they were worth it. We thought moving to India might be better, or going back to nursing school. Doing something with the handicapped or working with our hands. No one ever acted on these impulses, despite their daily, sometimes hourly, contractions. Instead we met in conference rooms to discuss the issues of the day.

Ordinarily jobs came in and we completed them in a timely and professional manner. Sometimes fuck ups did occur. Printing errors, transposed numbers. Our business was advertising and details were important. If the third number after the second hyphen in a client's toll-free number was a six instead of an eight, and if it went to print like that, and showed up in *Time* magazine, no one reading the ad could call now and order today. No matter that they could go to the web site, we still had to eat the price of the ad. Is this boring you yet? It bored us every day. Our boredom was ongoing, a collective boredom, and it would never die because

131

we would never die.

Lynn Mason was dying of cancer. She was a partner in the agency. Dying? It was uncertain. She was in her early forties. Breast cancer. No one could identify exactly how everyone had come to know this fact. Was it a fact? Some people called it rumor. But in fact there was no such thing as rumor. There was fact, and then there was what did not come up in conversation. Breast cancer was controllable if caught in the early stages but Lynn may have waited too long. We recalled looking at Frank Brizzolera and thinking he had six months, tops. Old Brizz, we called him. He smoked like a fiend. He stood outside the building in the most inclement weather, absorbing Old Golds in nothing but a sweater vest. Then and only then, he looked indomitable. When he returned inside, nicotine stink preceded him as he walked down the hall, where it lingered long after he entered his office. He began to cough, and from our own offices we heard the working-up of solidified lung sediment. Some people put him on their Celebrity Death Watch every year because of the coughing, even though he wasn't an official celebrity. He knew it, too, he knew he was on death watch, and that certain wagering individuals would profit from his death. He knew it because he was one of us, and we knew everything.

We didn't know who was stealing things from other people's workstations. Always small items—postcards, framed photographs. We had our suspicions but no proof. We believed it was probably being done not for the loot so much as the excitement—the shoplifter's addictive kick, or maybe it was a pathological cry for attention. Hank Neary, one of the agency's only black writers, asked, "Come on—who could want my travel toothbrush?"

We didn't know who was responsible for putting the sushi roll behind Joe Pope's bookshelf. The first couple of days Joe had no clue about the sushi. Then he started taking furtive sniffs at his pits, and holding the wall of his palm to his mouth to get blowback from his breath. By the end of the week, he was certain it wasn't him. We were smelling it, too. Persistent, high in the nostrils, it became worse than a dying animal. Joe's gorge rose every time he entered his office. The following week the smell was so atrocious the building people got involved, hunting the office for what turned out to be a sunshine roll—tuna, whitefish, salmon, and sprouts. Mike Boroshansky, the chief of security, kept bringing his tie up to his nose, as if he were a real cop at the scene of a murder.

We thanked each other. It was customary after every exchange. Our thanks were never disingenuous or ironic. We said thanks for getting this done so quickly, thanks for putting in so much effort. We had a meeting and when a meeting was over, we said thank you to the meeting-makers for having made the meeting. Very rarely did we say anything negative or derogatory about meetings. We all knew there was a good deal of pointlessness to nearly all the meetings and in fact one meeting out of every three or four was nearly perfectly without gain or purpose but many meetings revealed the one thing that was necessary and so we attended them and afterward we thanked each other.

Karen Woo always had something new to tell us and we hated her guts for it. She would start talking and our eyes would glaze over. Might it be true, as we sometimes feared on the commute home, that we were callous, unfeeling individuals, incapable of sympathy, and full of spite toward people for no reason other than their proximity and familiarity? We had these sudden revelations that we were far from our better selves. Should we quit? Would that solve it? Or were those qualities innate, dooming us to nastiness and paucity of spirit? We hoped not.

Marcia Dwyer became famous for sending an e-mail to Genevieve Latko-Devine. Marcia often wrote to Genevieve after meetings. "It is really irritating to work with irritating people," she wrote once. There she ended it and waited for Genevieve's response. Usually when she heard back from Genevieve, instead of writing her again, which would take too long—Marcia was an art director, not a writer—she would head down to Genevieve's office, close the door, and the two women would talk. The only thing bearable about the irritating event involving the irritating person was the thought of telling it all to Genevieve, who would understand better than anyone else. Marcia could have called her mother, her mother would have listened. She could have called one of her four brothers, any one of those South side crowbars would have been more than happy to beat up the irritating person. But they would not have understood. They would have sympathized, but that was not the same thing. Marcia needed understanding, and Genevieve would only need to nod for Marcia to know that she was getting through. Did we not all understand the essential need for someone to understand? But the e-mail Marcia got back was not from Genevieve. It was from Jim Jackers. "Are you talking about me?" he wrote. Amber Ludwig wrote, "I'm not Genevieve." Benny Shassburger wrote, "I think you goofed." Tom Mota wrote, "Ha!" Marcia was mortified. She got sixty-five e-mails in two minutes. One from HR cautioned her about the dangers of sending private e-mails. Jim wrote a second time. "Can you please tell me—is it me, Marcia? Am I the irritating person you're talking about?"

Marcia wanted to eat Jim's heart because some mornings he shuffled up to the elevators and greeted us by saying, "What up, my niggas?" He meant it ironically in an effort to be funny but he was just not the man to pull it off. It made us cringe, especially Marcia, especially if Hank was present.

In those days it was rare that someone pushed someone else down the hall really fast in a swivel chair. Most of the time there were long, long pauses during which we could hear ourselves breathe as we bent over our individual desks, working on some task at hand, lost to ourselves—a long pause before Benny, bored, came and stood in the doorway. "What are you doing?" he'd ask.

It could have been any of us. "Working," was the usual reply.

Then Benny would tap his topaz class ring on the doorway and drift away.

How we hated our coffee mugs! Our mouse pads, our desk clocks, our daily calendars, all the contents of our desk drawers. Even the photos of our loved ones taped to our computer monitors for uplift and support turned to cloying reminders of time served. But when we got a new office, a bigger office, and we brought everything with us into the new office, how we loved everything all over again, and thought hard about where to place things, and looked with satisfaction at the end of the day at how well our old things looked in this new, improved, important space. There was no doubt in our minds just then that we had made all the right decisions, whereas most days we were men and women of two minds. Everywhere you looked, in the hallways and bathrooms, the coffee bar and cafeteria, the lobbies and the print stations, there we were with our two minds.

There seemed to be only the one electronic pencil sharpener in the whole damn place. ✶

MAY 2006

I have a bookshelf over my bed, which is where I put the Books Bought and others that I have a serious intention of reading one day. And inevitably, over time, some of these are pronounced dead, and taken gently and respectfully downstairs either to the living room shelves, if they are hardbacks, or the paperback bookcase immediately outside the bedroom door, where they are allowed to rest in peace. (Do we have a word for something that looked like a good idea once? I hope so.) I'm sure you all knew this, but in fact books never die—it's just that I am clearly not very good at finding a pulse. I have learned this from my two younger children, who have taken to pulling books off the shelves within their reach and dropping them on the floor. Obviously I try not to notice, because noticing might well entail bending down to pick them up. But when I have finally and reluctantly concluded that no one else is going to do it, the book or books in my hand frequently look great—great and unread—and they are thus returned to the bookshelf over the bed. It's a beautiful, if circular, system, something like the process of convectional rainfall: interest evaporates, and the books are reduced to so much hot air, so they rise, you know, sideways, or even downstairs, but then blah blah and they fall to the ground... something like, anyway, although perhaps not exactly like.

This is precisely how Michael Ondaatje's *Running in the Family* was recently rediscovered. It turns out that I own a beautiful little Bloomsbury Classics hardback, as attractive to a small child, clearly, as it was to me. Indeed it's so attractive that it wasn't even placed back on the bookshelf over the bed: I began reading it fresh off the floor, as if it weren't rainfall after all, but a ripe, juicy... enough with the inoperable imagery. *Running in the Family* is a fever dream of a book, delirious, saturated with color; it's a travel book, and a family history, and a memoir, and it's funny and unforgettable. Ondaatje grew up in Sri Lanka, then called Ceylon, and it would not be unkind to describe his father as nuts—now and again, dangerously so. He pretended to have gone to Cambridge University (he sailed to England, stayed in Cambridge for the requisite three years, read a lot, and hung out with students without ever bothering to enroll); he was banned from the Ceylon Railways after hijacking a train, knocking out his traveling companion, who happened to be the future Prime Minister of the country, and bringing the entire railway system to a standstill; he was a part-time alcoholic, prone to epic drinking bouts, who buried scores of bottles of gin in the back garden for emergencies.

Ondaatje helps us to float over all this emotional landscape so that it feels as if we were viewing it from a hot-air balloon on a perfect day; someone with a different temperament (or someone much younger, someone who still felt raw) could have written— and been forgiven for writing—something darker and more troubling. "I showed what you had written to someone and they laughed and said what a wonderful childhood we must have had, and I said it was a nightmare," says an unnamed sibling at the end of the book, which tells you pretty much all you need to know about the theory and practice of memoir: it ain't the meat, it's the motion. The passage describing the death of Lalla, Ondaatje's grandmother, who was swept away in a flood, is one of the most memorable accounts of someone's last moments that I can remember. I'm grateful to my children for all sorts of things, of course, things that will inevitably come to me immediately after I have finished this column and sent it off; but I'm extremely grateful that one of them dropped this wonderful book on the floor. Actually, that may well be it, in terms of what my sons have given me, which puts a different complexion on the experience. I loved *Running in the Family,* and I mean the author no disrespect. But it's not much to show for twelve years of fatherhood, really, is it?

I've been losing a lot of books recently, so I am glad that nature has been bountiful, whether that bounty takes the form of fruit or rain. I have no idea where I've put *Eustace and Hilda,* the L. P. Hartley trilogy I was reading and loving, and Andrew Smith's book about the Apollo astronauts, *Moondust,* which I started and stopped a while back, was missing for most of this month, and as a consequence I haven't quite finished it. (It turned up in a drawer.) Lots of people are reading it here at the moment—it's a Richard and Judy book, Richard and Judy being our equivalent of Oprah— which is both weird and great, because in many ways *Moondust* is an eccentric book, with a set of references (Bowie, Neil Young, Updike, Rufus Wainwright, Eric Hobsbawm) that perfectly reflect the author's interests without necessarily reflecting the tastes of a mass reading public.

Smith knows that his obsession with the moon landings is about something else, and he is particularly good at teasing out the personal and global meanings of the Apollo missions—hell, there are even a few cosmic meanings in there—without ever sounding mad or pretentious. The author argues that when Apollo died in 1972, the dreams of the '60s died with it (and David Bowie is quoted as saying that the '70s were the start of the twenty-first century, which means that the twentieth century, perhaps uniquely, contained only seven decades), and there's a nostalgia for what the future used to represent and no longer can, and there's all sorts of stuff about aging and ambition. Despite the astronauts' protestations to the contrary, it's clearly been a struggle, flying to the moon and back in your thirties and forties, and then having to live out the rest of your life earthbound.

There's something in *Moondust* that I'd never thought about before, and it's haunted me ever since I read it. I had always felt rather sorry for Michael Collins, Richard Gordon, and the other four guys who flew all the way to the moon but then had to stay in the Command Module. I'd always had them down as close-but-no-cigar Pete Best types, doomed to be remembered for all time as unlucky. And yet their Apollo mission was surely every bit as extraordinary as those of the guys who got to put up flags and drive around in little golf buggies: forty-seven minutes of each lunar orbit that the Command Module took was spent on the far side of the moon, "out of sight and unreachable and utterly, utterly alone." The six Pete Bests were, as one NASA employee put it, the loneliest men "since Adam." Charles Lindbergh actually wrote to Collins, saying that walking on the moon was all very well, "but it seems to me that you had an experience of in some ways greater profundity." I find that it takes most of my courage simply to contemplate their pitch-black solitude. The closest I have ever come, I think, was last Christmas Day, when I walked round the corner to buy cigarettes and my whole neighborhood was utterly deserted. I'm not suggesting for a moment that my existential terror rivalled theirs, but it was a pretty creepy couple of minutes, and I was certainly glad to see the guy in the shop.

There are now nine people in the world who have walked on the moon, and unless something dramatic happens (and I'm talking about a governmental rethink rather than a cure for death), it won't be too long before there is none. That might not mean anything to a lot of you, because you are, I am led to understand, young people, and the moonwalks didn't happen in your lifetime. (How can you be old enough to read the *Believer* and not old enough to have seen Neil Armstrong live? What's happening to the world?) But it means a lot to me, and Andrew Smith, and when the Apollo missions, the future as we understood it, become history, then something will be lost from our psyches. But what do you care? Oh, go back to your hip-hop and your computer games and your promiscuity. (Or your virginity. I forget which one your generation is into at the moment.)

Kurt Vonnegut's *A Man Without a Country* was an oddly fitting companion to Smith's book, perhaps because the quirky humanist hope that one used to discern in Vonnegut's novels—several of which were written just as men were trying to get to the moon, and which frequently took an extraterrestrial view of our planet—is all but extinguished here. It's a charming, funny, wise little book, of course, because Vonnegut is incapable of writing anything that doesn't possess these qualities, but it's sad, too. Perhaps the questionable advantage of old age—Vonnegut is in his eighties now—is that you can see that hope is chimerical, and *A Man Without a Country* is devastatingly gloomy about the mess we have made of the world. I know he's right, but there is something in me, something callow and unrealistic (and something connected with the little boys who pull books off the shelves and drop them on the floor), that stops me from *feeling* that he's right. It has a very good smoking joke in it, though, this book. "Here's the news," says Vonnegut. "I am going to sue the Brown & Williamson Tobacco Company, manufacturers of Pall Mall cigarettes, for a billion bucks! Starting when I was only twelve years old, I have never chain-smoked anything but unfiltered Pall Malls. And for many years now, right on the package, Brown and Williamson have promised to kill me. But I am now eighty-two. Thanks a lot, you dirty rats."

It's been kind of a gloomy month, all in all, because Marjane Satrapi's two brilliant, heartbreaking graphic novels, *Persepolis: The Story of a Childhood* and *Persepolis 2: The Story of a Return,* aren't likely to lift the spirits, either. The story of Satrapi's childhood is also the story of the Iranian revolution, so she witnessed one violent and repressive regime replacing another; I got the same feeling I had while reading Jung Chang's *Wild Swans,* that the events described are so fantastical, so surreal and horrific, that they no longer seem to belong to the real world but to some metaphorical Orwellian dystopia. We know very little of the real world, though, those of us who live in the U.S. and Europe, just our small and relatively benign corner of it, and though we can see that the Guardians of the Revolution are human, just like us, it's pretty hard to find a way in to their humanity. Satrapi follows the trail of blood that leads from the overthrow of the Shah, through the fatuous and tragic war with Iraq, and on to the imprisonment, torture, and eventual murder of the leftists who helped bring about his downfall. And as the free-thinking daughter of left-leaning parents, Satrapi is able to use the small frames of her own life to create the bigger picture without contrivance or omission. (If the first book is slightly more successful than the second, it's because Satrapi spent some of the 1980s in Austria, so her personal and national histories take divergent paths.)

Satrapi draws in stark black-and-white blocks which bring to mind some of Eric Gill's woodcuts, and these blocks quickly begin to make perfect sense; in fact, it would be pretty hard not to draw postrevolutionary Iran without them—what with the beards and the robes and the veils, there was and still is a lot of black around. You know how bad things were for young Marjane and her mates? A poster of Kim Wilde comes to represent freedom, and who wants to live in a place where that's been allowed to happen? I know myself well enough to understand that I would never have read a prose memoir describing this life and these events— I wouldn't have wanted to live with this amount of fear and pain over days and weeks. I'm glad I understand more than I did, though, and these books, it seems to me, provide an object lesson in all that's good about graphic novels.

I picked up Bernard Levin's *The Pendulum Years*, about Britain in the '60s, because there's a little story in it that I'd always thought would make a good film, and I wanted to remind myself of the details. But then I remembered that the book contained one of my favorite pieces of comic writing, Levin's account of the Lady Chatterley trial, so I reread that, and a few of the other chapters. The piece on the Lady Chatterley trial made me laugh all over again, but it struck me this time that, even though Levin does a great job, it's not so much his writing that's funny as the trial itself; it's hard to go wrong with this material. For the benefit of young people: at the beginning of the 1960s, Penguin Books published Lawrence's *Lady Chatterley's Lover*, the first time it had been available to the general public since 1928, and the publishers were promptly prosecuted. Penguin won the ensuing court case, but not before some very English (and, it has to be said, extremely dim) lawyers argued, with unintentional comic élan, that the book had no literary merit, and therefore Penguin couldn't justify its obscene content. The law's notion of literary merit was both revealing and instructive—Mr. Griffith-Jones, for the prosecution, doubted, for example, that any book which contains a misquotation from the Twenty-fourth Psalm could be said to be much good. "Do you not think that in a work of high literary merit... he might take the trouble to look it up?"

Mr. Griffith-Jones was also perturbed by Lawrence's repeated use of the words *womb* and *bowels,* taking the view that your absolutely top authors, your greats, if you will, would get the thesaurus out. "Then a little bit further down page 141, towards the bottom, at the end of the longish paragraph the two words 'womb' and 'bowels' appear again…. Is that really what you call expert, artistic writing?" This really happened, honestly.

I was going to point out the bleeding obvious (as I prefer to do whenever possible, because it takes less effort, but fills up the space anyway)—I was going to say that a decade that began like this ended with man walking on the moon. Things aren't quite that cheerily progressive, though, are they? Because we're not landing men on the moon, or anywhere else in space—indeed, we no longer even possess the proper technology. There are plenty of people out there, however, who don't want us reading about wombs and bowels. Just ask Marjane Satrapi. ✲

A *selection from*

PERSEPOLIS

by MARJANE SATRAPI

✮ ✮ ✮

IN NO TIME, THE WAY PEOPLE DRESSED BECAME AN IDEOLOGICAL SIGN. THERE WERE TWO KINDS OF WOMEN.

THE FUNDAMENTALIST WOMAN

THE MODERN WOMAN

YOU SHOWED YOUR OPPOSITION TO THE REGIME BY LETTING A FEW STRANDS OF HAIR SHOW.

THERE WERE ALSO TWO SORTS OF MEN.

THE FUNDAMENTALIST MAN

BEARD — SHIRT HANGING OUT

THE PROGRESSIVE MAN

SHAVED, WITH OR WITHOUT MUSTACHE — SHIRT TUCKED IN

ISLAM IS MORE OR LESS AGAINST SHAVING.

BUT LET'S BE FAIR. IF WOMEN FACED PRISON WHEN THEY REFUSED TO WEAR THE VEIL, IT WAS ALSO FORBIDDEN FOR MEN TO WEAR NECKTIES (THAT DREADED SYMBOL OF THE WEST). AND IF WOMEN'S HAIR GOT MEN EXCITED, THE SAME THING COULD BE SAID OF MEN'S BARE ARMS. AND SO, WEARING SHORT-SLEEVED SHIRTS WAS ALSO FORBIDDEN.

THERE WAS A KIND OF JUSTICE, AFTER ALL.

IT WASN'T ONLY THE GOVERNMENT THAT CHANGED. ORDINARY PEOPLE CHANGED TOO.

LOOK AT HER! LAST YEAR SHE WAS WEARING A MINISKIRT, SHOWING OFF HER BEEFY THIGHS TO THE WHOLE NEIGHBORHOOD. AND NOW MADAME IS WEARING A CHADOR. IT SUITS HER BETTER, I GUESS.

AS FOR HER FUNDAMENTALIST HUSBAND WHO DRANK HIMSELF INTO A STUPOR EVERY NIGHT, NOW HE USES MOUTHWASH EVERY TIME HE UTTERS THE WORD "ALCOHOL."

AND THEIR SON SAYS HE PRAYS EVERY DAY!

IF ANYONE EVER ASKS YOU WHAT YOU DO DURING THE DAY, SAY YOU PRAY, YOU UNDERSTAND??

OK...

AT FIRST, IT WAS A LITTLE HARD, BUT I LEARNED TO LIE QUICKLY.

I PRAY FIVE TIMES A DAY.

ME? TEN OR ELEVEN TIMES... SOMETIMES TWELVE.

JUNE/JULY 2006

BOOKS BOUGHT:

* *Sons of Mississippi*
  —Paul Hendrickson
* *Last Days of Summer*
  —Steve Kluger
* *True Adventures with the King
  of Bluegrass*—Tom Piazza
* *On Fire*—Larry Brown
* *The Devil's Highway*
  —Luis Alberto Urrea
* *Happiness*
  —Darrin M. McMahon
* *The Mysterious Secret of the
  Valuable Treasure*
  —Jack Pendarvis

BOOKS READ:

* *Into the Wild*
  —Jon Krakauer
* *The Boy Who Fell Out of the
  Sky*—Ken Dornstein
* *The March*—E. L. Doctorow
* *Freakonomics*
  —Steven D. Levitt
  & Stephen J. Dubner

Last month I read Marjane Satrapi's two Persepolis books and Kurt Vonnegut's *A Man Without a Country*, and I seem to recall that I described the experience as somewhat gloomy. Ha! That was nothing! I didn't know I was born! I now see that the time I spent in Satrapi's horrific postrevolutionary Iran, and the time I gave over to Vonnegut telling us that the world is ending, were the happiest days of my life. The end of the world? Bring it on! With the honorable exception of *Freakonomics,* the most cheerful book I read this month was Jon Krakauer's *Into the Wild,* the story of how and why a young man walked into the Alaskan wilderness and starved (or perhaps poisoned) himself to death. *Into the Wild* wins the Smiley Award because it has a body count of one. Ken Dornstein's memoir *The Boy Who Fell Out of the Sky* begins and ends with the Lockerbie disaster in 1988, when a Pan Am plane blew up over a Scottish village, killing all 259 passengers, including the author's older brother David. And E. L. Doctorow's novel *The March* describes William Sherman's journey from Atlanta up to North Carolina, and just about everybody dies, some of them in ways that you don't want to spend a long time thinking about.

I was actually in North Carolina when I finished *The March*—this is something I like to do when I'm particularly enjoying a novel, despite the cost. (Did you know that there's no such planet as Titan? Vonnegut just made it up. They could have put that on the jacket, no? Oh well. You live and learn.) A couple of days later I passed the book on to one of my travelling companions, Dave Bielanko of the mighty band Marah, and he in return gave me the Krakauer book. It's what you do when you're on the road. Oh, yeah. There's a lot of, like, brotherhood and stuff. We were actually on the road between Memphis, Tennessee, and Oxford, Mississippi, a journey that takes approximately ninety minutes, and those ninety minutes were the only chunk of road I experienced. But never mind! I was there, swapping books, and, you know, looking out of the window. (And Oxford, Mississippi, is yet another place in the U.S. that I want to move to. Everyone there is a writer, or a musician, or someone who hasn't yet bothered doing either thing but could if he or she wanted to. And the mayor runs the bookstore, and in Faulkner's house you can read the plot outline he wrote in pencil on the wall, and you can see the can of dog repellent he kept by his desk, and the sun shines a lot.)

It's a strange experience, reading Ken Dornstein's memoir immediately after I'd finished *Into the Wild,* because there were occasions when it seemed as though Dornstein and Krakauer were writing about the same young man. Here's Chris McCandless, the doomed explorer, at college: "During that final year in Atlanta, Chris had lived off campus in a monkish room furnished with little more than a thin mattress on the floor, milk crates and a table." And here's David Dornstein: "David's room was a classic writer's Spartan cell—a desk, a chair, a mattress on the floor, books stacked all around." Both David Dornstein and McCandless spend an awful lot of time underlining meaningful passages in classic literature; these passages will later be discovered by future biographers, and both of these young men seemed to presume that there would be future biographers, because they left hundreds of pages of notes. David Dornstein, who wanted passionately to write, frequently imagines that his future biographer will have to piece together his work from these notes (chillingly, more than once he imagines himself killed in a plane crash); McCandless refers to himself in the pseudonymous third person—he was "Alexander Supertramp." Both of them have a taste for a slightly affected mock-heroic voice. And both of them seem doomed.

David Dornstein wasn't doomed in the same way as Chris McCandless, of course. McCandless chose to walk almost entirely unequipped into deadly terrain in order to live out some half-baked neurotic Thoreau fantasy. David Dornstein simply got on a routine passenger flight from London to New York, but what is remarkable about Ken Dornstein's memoir is that his brother's tragic and ungovernable fate seems like an organic part of the story he's telling. Someone sent me a proof copy of *The Boy Who Fell Out of the Sky* a while back, and I didn't think I was going to read it, partly because I couldn't imagine how it could be a *book*. To put it crudely and brutally, my anticipated problem was all in the title: whatever David's story was, it would be ended by a random, senseless explosion. (I'd been afraid of exactly the same thing with my brother-in-law's novel *Pompeii*—how can you create a narrative arc when you're just going to dump a load of lava on people's heads?) I don't know whether it's tasteless to say that the end of his life makes sense, but that's the unlikely trick that his brother pulls off.

Creating narrative coherence out of awful accident is, I suppose, a textbook way of dealing with this sort of grief (and grief, of course, is mostly what this book is about). It's partly Dornstein's skill as a writer that makes the raw material seem tailor-made for the form he has chosen, but the lives examined here are also freakishly appropriate for this kind of examination. It's not just the notes that his brother left, the half-finished stories and abandoned novels and instructions to literary executors, the letter to David from his father that explains and explores the story of Daedalus and Icarus. Ken ends up married to David's college girlfriend, but before they get there the two of them have to work out, slowly and painfully, whether there's any more to their relationship than a shared loss. And David wanted Ken to become the writer he feared he would never be, so the very existence of *The Boy Who Fell Out of the Sky* provides another layer of complication. It's a compelling, sad, thoughtful book, and I'm glad I picked it up.

Sixty passengers killed in the Lockerbie bombing fell onto the roof and garden of one particular house in the town. (The woman who lived there, perhaps understandably, moved away.) We can't imagine horror on that scale intruding into our domestic lives, but in Doctorow's novel *The March* it happens all the time. A still, hot morning, everything in its place, and then suddenly the sound and soon the sight of an avenging army come to fuck up everything you own and hold dear, and then the flames, and quite often something worse on top. And of course one has every right to be troubled by everything being held dear Down There, but this needn't prevent a sense of wonder at the sheer scale and energy of the devastation. (One of the things I kept thinking as I read the novel was, How on earth did you manage to create a country out of this mess?) In Doctorow's novel, Sherman's march absorbs turncoat soldiers just trying to get through, and freed slaves, and bereft

Southern widows, and cold-eyed surgeons; they're all eaten up and digested without a second thought. The violence, and violence of feeling, in this novel is on occasions so intense that it becomes kind of metaphysical, in the way that the violence in *King Lear* is metaphysical; the pitiful soldier with a spike protruding from his skull who has no memory of any kind, who lives every single second in the now, takes on an awful weight of meaning. And he ends up killing himself in the only way he can.

Lincoln turns up at the end of the book, as he has to, and in Chapel Hill, North Carolina, I bought a used copy of his letters and speeches. He must have been an annoying person to live with, no? Yes, there's the Gettysburg address. But there's also this letter to a young family friend: "I have scarcely felt greater pain in my life than on learning from Bob's letter, that you had failed to enter Harvard University.... *I know not how to aid you...*" [itals mine]. Come on, Abe! Is that really true? You couldn't pick up the phone for a pal? You can take this "honest" stuff too far, you know.

It would be easy, if unfair, to parody the post-Gladwell school of essays (and it's not unfair to say that *The Tipping Point* and *Blink* both paved the way for *Freakonomics*). You take two dissimilar things, prove—to your own satisfaction, at least—that they are not only not dissimilar but in fact more or less indistinguishable, suddenly cut away to provide some historical context, and then explain what it all means to us in our daily lives. So it goes something like this:

> On the face of it, World War II and Pamela Anderson's breasts would seem to have very little in common. And yet on closer examination, the differences seem actually much less interesting than the similarities. Just as World War II has to be seen in the context of the Great War that preceded it, it's not possible to think about Pammie's left breast without also thinking about her right. Pamela Anderson's breasts, like World War II, have both inspired reams of comment and

analysis, and occupied an arguably disproportionate amount of the popular imagination (in a survey conducted by the American Bureau of Statistical Analysis, more than 67 percent of men aged between thirty-five and fifty admitted to thinking about both World War II and what Anderson has under her T-shirt "more than once a year"); both World War II and the Anderson chest are becoming less *au courant* than they were. There are other, newer wars to fight; there are other, younger breasts to look at. What does all this tell us about our status as humans in the early years of the twenty-first century? To find out, we have to go back to the day in 1529 when Sir Thomas More reluctantly replaced Cardinal Wolsey as Lord Chancellor in Henry VIII's court....

They're always fun to read (the real essays, I mean, not my parody, which was merely fun to write, and a waste of your time). They pep you up, make you feel smart but a little giddy, occasionally make you laugh. *Freakonomics* occasionally hits you a little too hard over the head with a sense of its own ingenuity. "Now for another unlikely question: what did crack cocaine have in common with nylon stockings?" (One of the things they shared, apparently, is that they were both addictive, although silk stockings were only "practically" addictive, which might explain why there are comparatively few silk stocking–related drive-by shootings.) The answer to the question of whether mankind is innately and universally corrupt "may lie in... bagels." (The dots here do not represent an ellipsis, but a kind of trumpeting noise.) Schoolteachers are like sumo wrestlers, real estate agents are like the Ku Klux Klan, and so on. I enjoyed the book, which is really a collection of statistical conjuring tricks, but I wasn't entirely sure of what it was about.

I don't think I have ever had so many books I wanted to read. I picked up a few things in U.S. bookstores; I was given a load of cool-looking books by interesting writers when I was in Mississippi and ordered one or two more (Larry Brown's *On Fire,* for example) when I came home. Meanwhile I still want to go back to L. P. Hartley's *Eustace and Hilda* trilogy, but Hartley seems too English at the moment. And I have a proof copy of the new Anne Tyler, and this young English writer David Peace has written a novel about 1974 as seen through the prism of Brian Clough's disastrous spell in charge at Leeds United. (Brian Clough was.... Leeds United were.... Oh, never mind.) So I'd better push on.

Except... a long time ago, I used to mention Arsenal, the football team I have supported for thirty-eight years, in these pages. Arsenal was occasionally called in to provide an excuse for why I hadn't read as much as I wanted to, but up until a month or so ago, they were rubbish, and I couldn't use them as an excuse for anything. They weren't even an excuse for a football team. Anyway, now they're—*we're*—good again. We have the semifinals of the Champions League coming up in a couple of weeks, for the first time in my life, and I can see books being moved onto the bench for the next few weeks. Ah, the old dilemma: books versus rubbish. (Or maybe, books versus stuff that can sometimes seem more fun than books.) It's good to have it back. ✭

Thanks to: Andrew Leland, Vendela Vida, Heidi Julavits and the Sprce, Zelda Turner, Tony Lacey, Joanna Prior, Rosie Gailer, and Caroline Dawnay. Thanks also to Nick Coleman, Sarah Vowell, DV DeVincentis, Wesley Stace, Harry Ritchie, Tony Quinn, Rachel Cooke, Eli Horowitz, Gill Hornby, Robert Harris, and everyone else who has recommended a book to me.

Grateful acknowledgment is made to the following for permission to reprint previously published material:

From PERSEPOLIS: THE STORY OF A CHILDHOOD by Marjane Satrapi, translated by Mattias Ripa & Blake Ferris, copyright © 2003 by L'Association, Paris, France. Used by permission of Pantheon Books, a division of Random House, Inc.

Pages 6-9 from Chapter One of CITIZEN VINCE by Jess Walter. Copyright © 2005 by Jess Walter. Reprinted by permission of HarperCollins Publishers.

AND THEN WE CAME TO THE END by Joshua Ferris is published in the U.S. by Little, Brown & Co (March 2007) and in the U.K. by Viking (April 2007). Reprinted by kind permission of Little, Brown and Company U.S. and Penguin Books U.K.

GHOSTING by Jennie Erdal was first published in Great Britain by Canongate Books Ltd, 14 High Street, Edinburgh, EH1 1TE. Reprinted by kind permission of Canongate.

ASSASSINATION VACATION by Sarah Vowell is published by Simon & Schuster Paperbacks, Rockefeller Center, 1230 Avenue of the Americans, New York, NY 10020. Reprinted by kind permission of Simon & Schuster.

Nick Hornby is the bestselling author of the novels *High Fidelity*, *About a Boy*, *How to Be Good*, and *A Long Way Down* (shortlisted for the 2005 Whitbread Novel of the Year Award), as well as the nonfiction *Fever Pitch*, *Songbook* (finalist for the National Book Critics Circle Award for criticism), and *The Polysyllabic Spree*, the first collection of his monthly column from the *Believer*. He lives in Highbury, North London, with his wife and three sons.

NICK HORNBY
WILL NOT STOP
READING

AND NEITHER
SHOULD YOU!

In addition to Nick Hornby's monthly column, every issue of the *Believer* features terrific essays from writers like Rick Moody, Paul Collins, and Michelle Tea, along with interviews with the likes of David Foster Wallace, George Saunders, Janet Malcolm, Shirley Hazzard, Ice Cube, Shirin Neshat, and Ashida Kim (who is a ninja). Maureen Howard called the *Believer* "a wealth of intelligence, energy, and wit." Don't miss a single issue!

visit us online at
www.believermag.com
and fill out the form below for a special discount!